THIRD EDITION

W9-AUK-315

My
Social Media
for Seniors

que
221 River Street
Hoboken, New Jersey 07030 USA

Real Possibilities

Michael Miller

My Social Media for Seniors, Third Edition

Copyright © 2020 by Pearson Education, Inc.

ISBN-13: 978-0-13-591163-1

ISBN-10: 0-13-591163-X

Library of Congress Control Number: on file

1 2019

Trademarks

All terms mentioned in this book that are known to be trademarks or service marks have been appropriately capitalized. Que Publishing cannot attest to the accuracy of this information. Use of a term in this book should not be regarded as affecting the validity of any trademark or service mark.

Unless otherwise indicated herein, any third-party trademarks that may appear in this work are the property of their respective owners and any references to third-party trademarks, logos, or other trade dress are for demonstrative or descriptive purposes only. Such references are not intended to imply any sponsorship, endorsement, authorization, or promotion of Que Publishing products by the owners of such marks, or any relationship between the owner and Que Publishing or its affiliates, authors, licensees, or distributors.

Warning and Disclaimer

Every effort has been made to make this book as complete and as accurate as possible, but no warranty or fitness is implied. The information provided is on an "as is" basis. The author and the publisher shall have neither liability nor responsibility to any person or entity with respect to any loss or damages arising from the information contained in this book.

Special Sales

For information about buying this title in bulk quantities, or for special sales opportunities (which may include electronic versions; custom cover designs; and content particular to your business, training goals, marketing focus, or branding interests), please contact our corporate sales department at corpsales@pearsoned.com or (800) 382-3419.

For government sales inquiries, please contact governmentsales@pearsoned.com.

For questions about sales outside the U.S., please contact intlcs@pearson.com.

Editor-in-Chief
Brett Bartow

Executive Editor
Laura Norman

Associate Editor
Chhavi Vig

Marketing
Stephane Nakib

Director, AARP Books
Jodi Lipson

Editorial Services
The Wordsmithery LLC

Managing Editor
Sandra Schroeder

Senior Project Editor
Tonya Simpson

Copy Editor
Charlotte Kughen

Indexer
Cheryl Lenser

Proofreader
Sarah Kearns

Technical Editor
Jeri Usbay

Editorial Assistant
Cindy Teeters

Cover Designer
Chuti Prasertsith

Compositor
Bronkella Publishing

Graphics
T J Graham Art

Contents at a Glance

Table of Contents

3 What to Share—and What *Not* to Share—on Social Media   **37**

About the Author

Michael Miller is a prolific and popular writer, known for his ability to explain complex topics to everyday readers. He has written more than 200 nonfiction books over the past three decades, with more than 1.5 million copies sold worldwide. He writes about a variety of topics, including technology, business, and music. His best-selling books for Que include *My TV for Seniors, My Facebook for Seniors, My iPad for Seniors, My Windows 10 Computer for Seniors, My Smart Home for Seniors, My Google Chromebook,* and *Computer Basics: Absolute Beginner's Guide.*

Find out more at the author's website: **www.millerwriter.com**

Follow the author on Twitter: **@molehillgroup**

Dedication

To Lloyd Short, my old friend and mentor, enjoy your final role.

Acknowledgments

Thanks to all the folks at Que who helped turn this manuscript into a book, including Laura Norman, Chhavi Vig, Charlotte Kughen, and technical editor Jeri Usbay. Thanks also to Jodi Lipson and the other good folks at AARP for supporting this and other books I've written.

Note: Most of the individuals pictured throughout this book are of the author himself, as well as friends and relatives (and sometimes pets). Some names and personal information are fictitious.

About AARP

AARP is a nonprofit, nonpartisan organization, with a membership of nearly 38 million, that helps people turn their goals and dreams into *real possibilities*™, strengthens communities, and fights for the issues that matter most to families such as healthcare, employment and income security, retirement planning, affordable utilities, and protection from financial abuse. Learn more at aarp.org.

We Want to Hear from You!

As the reader of this book, *you* are our most important critic and commentator. We value your opinion and want to know what we're doing right, what we could do better, what areas you'd like to see us publish in, and any other words of wisdom you're willing to pass our way.

We welcome your comments. You can email or write to let us know what you did or didn't like about this book—as well as what we can do to make our books better.

Please note that we cannot help you with technical problems related to the topic of this book.

When you write, please be sure to include this book's title and author as well as your name and email address. We will carefully review your comments and share them with the author and editors who worked on the book.

Email: community@informit.com

Reader Services

Register your copy of *My Social Media for Seniors* at www.informit.com/register for convenient access to downloads, updates, and corrections as they become available. To start the registration process, go to quepublishing.com/register and log in or create an account*. Enter the product ISBN, 9780135911631, and click Submit.

*Be sure to check the box that you would like to hear from us in order to receive exclusive discounts on future editions of this product.

Figure Credits

Various screenshots taken from social media websites are protected by their respective copyrights:

© AARP

© Facebook, Inc.

© Flickr

© Friendster

© Goodreads, Inc.

© 2018 Google LLC, used with permission. Google and the Google logo are registered trademarks of Google LLC.

© Instagram, Inc.

© LinkedIn Corporation

© Pinterest, Inc.

© Reddit, Inc.

© Microsoft Corporation

© Snap, Inc.

© Tumblr, Inc.

© Twitter

© YouTube

Permission is granted for use of images from the following sources:

Figure 2-1: Courtesy of The Burrad Street Journal

Figure 2-2: Courtesy of Real News Right Now

Figure 2-3: Courtesy of Natural News

Figure 2-4: Courtesy of Empire News

Figure 2-5: Courtesy of Snopes

Figure 2-6: Courtesy of Media Bias/Fact Check

Some photographs are owned by and used with permission from the following sources:

Figures 1-3, 3-2, 3-7: Courtesy of Dinah Lance

Figure 5-8: Courtesy of Steve Weiss

Figure 5-10: Courtesy of Alan Douglas Bower

Figure 5-12: Courtesy of NASA

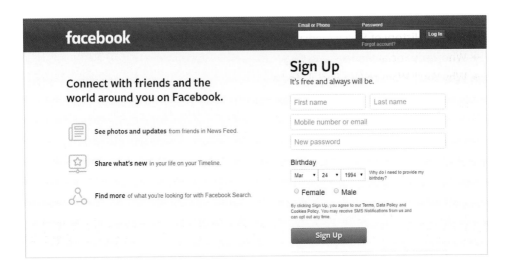

In this chapter, you learn all about social media—what they are, how they work, and why you might want to use them.

→ Understanding Social Media
→ A Short History of Social Media
→ Who Uses Social Media—and Why
→ Why You'll Want to Use Social Media

What Social Media Are—and Why We Use Them

You've heard people talking about this thing called *social media*. Chances are, some of your friends, family, and colleagues use Facebook, LinkedIn, Pinterest, Twitter, or some similar site. You might even have your own social media presence. (Facebook is especially popular among our generation.)

The term *social media* might sound complicated or technical or even a little confusing. Don't worry; it isn't. In reality, social media help you connect with your family, friends, and colleagues. It's a way to communicate with people you know and people you might like to know. And it's all done on your computer or smartphone or tablet, over the Internet.

Understanding Social Media

What exactly are—or is it *is*?—social media? There are lots of different definitions, but they all hinge on that one word: *social*.

Defining Social Media

Merriam-Webster defines social media as "forms of electronic communication… through which users create online communities to share information, ideas, personal messages, and other content."[*]

That's pretty technical. I like to think of social media as websites, apps, and services that host a community of users and make it easy for those users to communicate with one another using their computers, smartphones, or tablets. That communication can involve sharing messages and information, as well as pictures and videos. It's all about being social and encouraging social interactions.

In most instances, these social interactions come in the form of *posts* or *status updates,* which are short messages that are posted for public viewing by all of that person's friends on the site.

A status update shared on Facebook

A social media post can be a text-only message or one that includes photographs, videos, and links to other web pages. Whatever form the media takes, it's all about sharing things—socially.

---

[*] By Permission. From Merriam-Webster.com ©2019 by Merriam-Webster, Inc.
    https://www.merriam-webster.com/dictionary/social media

What's in a Name?

What some people call *social media* others call *social networks*. Both names refer to the same thing. That is, a social network is social media, and vice versa. So don't get hung up on the name.

Understanding How Social Media Works

For most people, social media are all about communicating and staying in touch with one another. It's the twenty-first-century way to let people know what you're up to—and to find out what everyone else is up to as well.

Of course, people were communicating and sharing things long before we ever heard of the Internet. We just used different media than we use today.

In the old, old days, the only way you found out what was going on was when someone wrote you a letter. That probably sounds quaint today, as letter writing is somewhat out of fashion. But I'm guessing you're old enough to have written a few letters in your time, so you know what I'm talking about.

Ah, the joys of receiving a letter from an old friend! I miss seeing a friend's address in the top-left corner, opening the envelope, and savoring the words within. Of course, most friends didn't write that often; writing was a lot of work, so you saved up your thoughts and experiences until you had a full letter's worth. But, man, it was great to read what your friends had been doing. It almost made the wait worthwhile.

That was then, and this is now. Today, nobody has the time or the patience or the attention span to write or read long letters. At some point back in the 1990s, email replaced the written letter as our primary means of correspondence. That wasn't necessarily a bad thing; emails were typically shorter than written letters, but you got them immediately—and you could respond to them immediately, too. With the Internet age came this faster and more direct form of communication, and we adapted to it.

For a lot of people today, however, email is old hat; it's too slow and takes too much time. Instead, most people nowadays prefer immediate communication, primarily (if not exclusively) via text messages on their phones and mobile devices.

The problem with text messages is that they're not centralized. If you're texting with a dozen friends, that's a dozen different "feeds" of information you have to keep track of. There's no central repository where you can read all your friends' messages in one place.

This is where social media comes in. Instead of writing a dozen (or a hundred) different letters or emails or texts to each of your friends telling them that you just bought a new pair of shoes (or car or house or whatever), you write a single post that those dozen (or hundred) different people can then read. Something happens, you write about it, it gets posted on the social networking site, and everyone you know can read about it. It takes all the work out of keeping your friends up to date on what you're doing.

Of course, it works in the other direction, too. Instead of waiting for letters or emails or text messages from each of your friends, you just log onto your friendly local social media site. There you find a feed of updates from everyone you know. Read the feed and you're instantly updated on what everyone is up to. That makes it really easy to keep in touch.

Now, social media let you do a lot more than just exchange status updates, but that's the most common activity and the reason most of us do the social media thing. Communications to and from all your friends, all in one place, all done from your personal computer or smartphone or tablet. It's like communications central for everyone you know—close friends or otherwise.

Building Social Communities

When you share your thoughts and interests via social media, you help to create online communities. To help facilitate this community building, many social media networks let you do more than exchange simple status updates. Depending on the social network, you might find some or all of the following features:

- **Public posts:** This is the heart and soul of social media. You post about something of interest, and all your friends on that social network read about it. (You also read the public posts from all your friends, of course.)

- **Private communications:** This can take the form of one-to-one private messaging, proprietary email service, and even live text messaging.

- **Video chat:** This is true face-to-face communications, in real time—assuming both parties have cameras on their personal computers, tablets, or smartphones, of course.

- **Groups and forums:** These are like online clubs built around specific areas of interest. You can find groups for hobbies like woodworking or quilting, for topics like politics or sports, and for just about anything else you can think of. There are even groups devoted to specific companies, schools, and entertainers. (Groups for entertainers are more like fan clubs than anything else.)

- **Photo and video sharing:** That's right, many social networks let you upload your pictures and movies and share them with all your friends on the network. It's the twenty-first-century way of sharing your photos—no slides or prints necessary.

There's a bit more than even all this, including event scheduling and the like, but you get the general idea. Social media *are* online communities and offer many of the same activities that you'd find in real-world communities.

A Short History of Social Media

The social media that we know today have been around for only about a decade—although their core features have existed since the earliest days of the Internet.

If you're old enough to remember the earliest personal computers back in the 1970s and 1980s, you may remember pre-Internet communications in the form of dial-up computer networks (such as America Online, CompuServe, and Prodigy), bulletin board systems (BBSs), and other simple online discussion forums. Well, these early online services served much the same function as do today's social media, offering topic-based discussion forums and chat rooms, just like Facebook and LinkedIn do today. What they didn't offer was a way to follow friends on the site or to publicly share status updates. But the seeds of today's social media were there.

Other components of modern social media developed after the rise of the public Internet and the World Wide Web. For example, numerous topic-based website communities, such as Classmates.com, Epicurious, and iVillage, arose in the mid-1990s. Personal blogs, which let users post short articles of information and opinion, emerged around the year 2000. And photo-sharing sites, such as Flickr and Photobucket, became a part of the Internet landscape in the early 2000s.

The first service to combine all of these features into a single social network was Friendster, in 2002. Friendster also introduced the concepts of "friends" and "friending" to the social web; it all came from the name, not surprisingly.

Friendster, the original social network

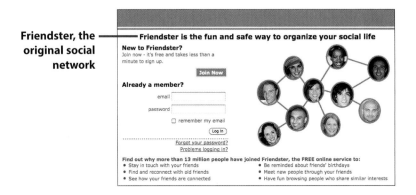

Friendster enjoyed immediate popularity (more than 3 million users within the first few months of operation), but ran into technical problems associated with that growth and was soon surpassed by MySpace, which launched the next year. MySpace became the Web's most popular social network in June 2006, and remained so for almost two years.

Friendster and MySpace were part of the first wave of social media. The second wave formed in 2004, when a site originally known as "thefacebook" came on the scene. What eventually became known as just "Facebook" was originally launched as a site where college students could socialize online, but it quickly opened its doors for users of all ages.

The Social Network

The story of Facebook's genesis was told in the 2010 film, *The Social Network*. Although some elements of the film are clearly fictitious, it's actually a fairly accurate retelling of events.

The broadening in Facebook's user base led to a huge increase in both users and usage, with Facebook surpassing MySpace in April 2008. Today, Facebook is not only the number-one social network, it's also the number-three site on the entire Internet, with more than 2.3 billion users of all ages. That's a pretty big deal.

Facebook, today's largest social network

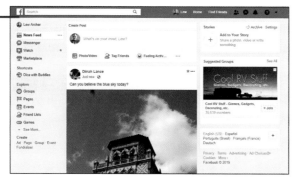

Facebook isn't the only social network today, however. Hot on its heels are several social media that are more specialized than the general-interest Facebook. These social media alternatives include Twitter (specializing in shorter, more immediate messages), Pinterest (which lets users share images they find all across the Internet), LinkedIn (targeting business professionals), and Instagram (which is all about photo and video sharing). None of these social media are near as big as Facebook, but they serve different needs.

Who Uses Social Media—and Why

With all that social media have to offer, it's not surprising that so many people use them day in and day out. As with many new technologies, social media started out being used almost exclusively by high school and college students. (That's how the Internet itself took off, after all.) But over time, social media spread from the young generation to the general public, including older users like you and me.

While different social media appeal to different groups of users, the audience for social media in general has evolved into something approximating that of the general population—which means that more and more older people are getting social. Taking Facebook as an example, 65% of U.S. adults aged 50 to 64 use Facebook, as do 41% of all people aged 65 and older. (These statistics come from Pew Research Center in 2018.)

Differing Popularity

Of course, not all social media are as popular with our generation. Twitter, for example, is used by just 8% of people aged 65 and older, and by 19% of those aged 50 to 64. (Twitter's largest group of users are those aged 18 to 29, 40% of whom use the service.)

In practice, then, social media such as Facebook appeal to all sorts of people who have all sorts of reasons for using the media:

- Friends and family members who want to keep in touch
- People looking for long-lost friends
- Business colleagues looking for collaboration and networking
- Singles who want to meet and match up with other singles
- Hobbyists looking for others who share their interests
- Classmates who need study partners and homework advice
- Musicians, actors, and celebrities (and politicians!) connecting with their fans

Plus anyone looking to keep up with the latest news and events—and share their opinions about those events. (Political opinions, especially.)

What all these types of users have in common is that they desire easy and immediate interaction with friends, family members, co-workers, and followers. With social media, it's easy to interact with other people via public posts, private communication, event calendars, and even community-based games and applications.

In short, the various social media available today help you keep in contact with large numbers of people without having to interact personally with each and every individual. It's effective and efficient communication.

>>>*Go Further*

DEMOGRAPHIC MIGRATION

I find it interesting that so many technologies are first adopted by younger users, but then use of the technologies eventually migrates upward and outward to older folks and the general population. That's how it happened not just with social media but also with other Internet-based technologies.

Take email, for instance. Email first became a thing back in the early 1990s, when students on college campuses got used to sending private messages to their friends over their schools' private email systems. They didn't want to give up their email when they graduated, which led them to seek out primitive email systems in the real world, including those connected to America Online and other commercial online services. This commercialization of email not only encouraged Hotmail and other companies to get into the email business but also nudged many large and small businesses to adopt email for their own intraoffice communications. Before you knew it, it wasn't just the college kids using email anymore; everybody, regardless of age, had an email address. It migrated upward from the kiddies to the adults.

It's been the same thing with social media. Friendster and MySpace had particular appeal to high school and college students, and Facebook was born on a college campus exclusively for the use of college students. It didn't take long, however, for these younger users to move out into the real world and take their love for (and reliance on) social media to a larger audience. Soon the twentysomethings became thirtysomethings, who communicated with fortysome-things, who dragged their fifty- and sixtysomething friends and relatives along for the ride. What started as a fun diversion for the younger generation became a useful means of sharing (and a fun diversion, too) for older generations.

So if you want to know what you and your friends will be using next, look to the high school and college kids. What they use today, we'll probably be using tomorrow.

Why You'll Want to Use Social Media

Whereas many younger users tend to sign in to a social network when they wake up in the morning and not sign out until they go to bed at night, older users tend not to be as obsessed with social media. We might check into Facebook or Pinterest a few times a day, but they don't monopolize our lives. Or at least they shouldn't.

Instead, most of us aged 50 and up tend to use social media on a more occasional basis to keep tabs on what friends, family members, and colleagues are up to. We are not typically as addicted to social media as our children and grandchildren are; we don't have to know what everyone is doing on a minute-by-minute basis. Instead, we can log in once or maybe twice a day and get the general drift of everyone's activities. That's enough information for most of us.

Grown-ups also use social media to reconnect with people we haven't seen in a while. A long while, sometimes. Personally, I use Facebook to check in with old friends from high school and college, and to reconnect with former colleagues and those I might want to work with again. (I guarantee you'll find people on Facebook and other social media that you haven't thought about for a long time—which might not always be a good thing, I suppose.)

Finding friends on Facebook

Social media are also a great way for family members—especially extended families—to keep abreast of comings and goings. It might take a lot of effort to personally write your cousins and aunts and uncles and nieces and nephews and stepchildren and in-laws and all the rest, but a single Facebook status update will do the job of multiple letters and emails. You can also use social media to share family photos with the rest of your family, which is a ton easier than printing and mailing photos manually.

Speaking of family members, social media are also great for keeping in touch with what your children and grandchildren are up to, without them actually having to have a conversation with you about it. All you have to do is add your kids to your social media friends lists, and you'll see all the posts they make public. (That's unless they adjust their privacy settings to exclude you from their most private thoughts, which if they're smart, they'll do.)

Of course, there are plenty of ways for adult users to waste time on social media, just as our kids do. I know a fair number of supposed grown-ups who get addicted to Candy Crush Saga and other social games, and spend way too much time playing them. Useless social media activity isn't the sole province of the young; we more mature users also can spend hours doing essentially nothing useful online.

Bottom line, those of us 50 and up use social media for many of the same reasons that younger folks do, but we use it in a smarter and less intrusive fashion. Or so we'd like to think, anyway.

In this chapter, you learn how various people and organizations use social media to disseminate false information—and how to recognize this type of fake news.

→ Why False Information Flourishes Online
→ How to Recognize Fake News, Propaganda, and Opinions Online
→ Some "Fake News" Is Real
→ How to Tell Real News from Fake News
→ How to Avoid Spreading Fake News

Separating Fact from Fiction Online

No doubt you've seen them online: headlines, news stories, links to web pages that make claims that don't feel quite right. Maybe it's something about the behavior of a given politician, or the details of some supposed new law, or even some wild claim that sounds more like a conspiracy theory than a news headline.

Chances are that what you're seeing isn't factual. It's what some people call "fake news"—a bunch of lies and hoaxes designed to fool the public into believing the unbelievable. And, if you're not careful, you can easily be duped by the latest round of falsehoods circulating on Facebook, Twitter, and other social media.

(WARNING: This chapter contains multiple examples of fake news, conspiracy theories, urban legends, and other unsavory topics. I apologize in advance for any offense these items may cause, but they're all to be found in social media online.)

Why False Information Flourishes Online

Just because someone posts something online doesn't mean it's true.

That last sentence is important, so please read it again:

Just because someone posts something online doesn't mean it's true.

If you remember nothing else from this chapter, remember that. Although the Internet can be a great source of news and information, it also can be a breeding ground for misinformation, lies, and propaganda. In fact, social media such as Facebook and Twitter exacerbate the problem, making it easier than ever before to spread rumor, innuendo, and plain old lies.

Spreading Lies—Online and Off

People have been spreading lies and propaganda forever. It's just that this sort of thing spreads faster today. It used to be that misinformation like this would be spread by word of mouth; a friend would tell another friend about some supposed thing happening, then that friend would tell somebody else, and eventually you'd hear about it. It took some time for the rumors and such to make their way throughout even a small community.

Today, however, all someone has to do is post the latest piece of misinformation on Facebook or Twitter, and literally seconds later it can spread around the entire planet. One influential person makes an ill-informed tweet and hundreds of thousands of people or more hear about it—and take it as the gospel truth. It gets even worse when some of these people pass on the original post to their online friends; pretty soon millions of people worldwide are exposed to the misinformation, and the original falsehood takes on a life of its own that is now difficult to dispute.

Going Viral

When a piece of information (or video or other type of file) gets circulated around a large number of people, it's said to have gone *viral*. The term comes from the way a biological virus spreads; on the Internet, anything that gets passed from person to person in this fashion resembles biological viral behavior.

This is how fake news becomes a real issue. It's especially prevalent in the world of politics, but it can permeate rational discussion in all fields of interest.

A Few Examples...

When we say fake news, what exactly are we talking about? There are variations on the theme (which we'll discuss later in this chapter), but I'm mainly talking about made-up, phony news stories, the kind you used to read in the weekly tabloid papers in the check-out lanes at your local grocery store. Now those fake stories are posted on fake websites and then shared on Facebook and other social media.

What kinds of fake stories are we talking about? Well, here are some of the top fake news headlines shared on Facebook in 2018, in no certain order:

- "Lottery Winner Arrested for Dumping $200,000 of Manure on Ex-Boss' Lawn"
- "Michael Jordan Resigns from the Board at Nike—Takes 'Air Jordans' with Him"
- "Donald Trump Ends School Shootings by Banning Schools"
- "North Korea Agrees to Open Its Doors to Christianity"

All of these stories were totally fake. Not a drop of truth in them.

Let's look at one such fake story in more detail. During the 2016 U.S. presidential election, a white supremacist Twitter account made the claim that the New York City Police Department had discovered the existence of a human-trafficking ring operating out of a Washington, DC-based pizzeria named Comet Ping Pong. This ring was supposedly tied to Democratic presidential candidate Hillary Clinton and her chief of staff, John Podesta.

This claim was, of course, totally fabricated. Although there is a pizza joint in Washington named Comet Ping Pong, it is not the headquarters for any human-trafficking operations, and Clinton and Podesta are not tied to the pizza parlor or any such unsavory operations.

The truth of the matter didn't stop the original tweet from being passed around online from person to person, and eventually being picked up by multiple right-wing message boards, Twitter feeds, and Facebook feeds. It even got top billing on many so-called fake news websites, which helped the unfounded rumor to spread even further and faster.

Before long, "Pizzagate," as the ruckus was ultimately dubbed, had to be addressed in the mainstream media. Many unwitting individuals believed what they heard and took to harassing the owners and staff of Comet Ping Pong online and in person. One such true believer even took it upon himself to personally visit the pizza place and fire off three rounds from an AR-15-style assault rifle. (Fortunately no one was hurt, and the perpetrator was arrested for his actions.)

And all this happened because one person posted something totally fabricated to his Twitter account. That's how fake news and innuendo spread and become truly dangerous online.

And a Few More...

The Pizzagate situation is just one (very prominent) example of fake news, and how it impacts people in the real world. I could cite hundreds of other examples, many of them political in nature, but many more related to other hot- and not-so-hot-button topics. Fake news sites have sprung up to muddy the waters about climate change, genetically modified food, gun violence, space travel, computer technology, racial issues, you name it. (And that's not counting the almost constant barrage of UFO and Bigfoot conspiracy theory sites.)

On the surface, much of this fake news is relatively harmless. (I mean, Bigfoot? Seriously?) But some of this false information could be deadly.

Take, for example, the topic of fake medical news. Yes, there are websites dispensing bogus medical advice, oftentimes pushing naturopathic and alternative cures in lieu of proven medical solutions. Fake news stories emanating from these sites have oozed across the Internet in recent years, many promising miracle cures that the medical establishment is, for some reason, hiding from the public.

If you've been on Facebook for any length of time, you've probably seen a few of these articles. Some of the more popular ones purport to offer a true cure for cancer, typically via some form of naturalistic treatment. One of my favorites has the headline, "Dandelion Weed Can Boost Your Immune System and Cure Cancer." Which, of course, it can't.

In every instance, the claims in these fake medical news articles have been dis-credited by doctors and healthcare researchers. Yet the fake stories persist, and people persist in reading and sometimes believing them.

This is not harmless folly. If you are a cancer victim and take these articles at face value, you might think you can stop your current expensive and often invasive treatments and switch to one of these holistic (and wholly disproven) solutions. Abandoning traditional medicine in favor of fake solutions could literally result in death.

Why Do People Believe Fake News?

On the surface, the claims that drive most fake news seem totally outrageous. Why, in the Pizzagate scenario, would a presidential candidate be involved with a human-trafficking operation—and from a small pizza joint, at that? Why would doctors knowingly squelch a miracle cure for cancer—and why would such a cure come from a common garden weed?

First, people tend to believe what they read online. We've been conditioned to trust the information provided by traditional newspaper and magazine journal-ists, so we don't automatically question similar information presented online. We want to believe what we read; we don't want to have to question everything.

Then there's what experts call "confirmation bias," which we all have to one degree or another. This is the tendency to interpret new information as confirma-tion of our existing beliefs. If we see something that aligns with what we already believe, we take it as further proof—whether it's true or not. Put another way, when someone introduces a new fact, we try to twist it around so that it seems to support our prior opinions. And if we can't, then we discount that new infor-mation as being somehow fake or illegitimate.

People also want to believe that there's hope. If you are the victim of a serious disease, you want to fervently believe that somewhere out there exists a pill, a treatment, an elixir you can take that will cure you. If you're deep in debt or can't find a job, you want to believe that the latest work-from-home scheme really does pay $40 per hour. We need to believe, and when conventional means offer little hope, we reach beyond. It's the same desperation that has fueled miracle cures and get-rich-quick schemes for generations.

When you combine fake news with the speed and efficiency of the Internet and social media, you amplify the problem. You see, one of the bad things about social media, and the Internet in general, is that you can filter it so that you only see those posts and stories that you want to see. You only have to visit those websites you want; you don't have to view any sites you don't like. The same thing with the news feeds you get on social media; you see the opinions of your friends and the people you follow, and don't see any the opinions of anyone else.

This also means that you tend to see the same stories and information multiple times. You might read the initial source of the information and then see that story reposted by one or more of your friends. The more often you see something, the more likely you are to view it as a fact—even if it isn't.

This all creates a kind of echo chamber, where you only hear from people and sources like you, and never get exposed to any opposing views. The echo chamber reinforces your existing views and never challenges them. You keep hearing more and more of the same thing, and less and less of anything remotely different—which can make you even more susceptible to fake news that buttresses what you already believe.

How to Recognize Fake News, Propaganda, and Opinions Online

So far we've discussed "fake news" in very general terms. In reality, there are many different types of false information disseminated online, and not all for the same purpose or effect.

Fake News

Let's start with fake news itself. Fake news is literally news stories that are deliberately false. These fake news stories are filled with lies and made-up "facts" about a particular topic. They describe events that didn't happen—or didn't happen the way the story describes.

In other words, fake news is fiction, in the form of a purportedly (but not really) real news article.

You find fake news stories in people's social media feeds, and on fake news web-sites. These are sites that exist purely to disseminate fake news articles—hoaxes, disinformation, and propaganda. The stories posted on these websites then get shared via social media, which is why you see them posted by your friends in your Facebook and Twitter news feeds.

The intent of these sites is to mislead people into thinking they're reading real news articles. They're neither satirical nor accidental. The writers are purposefully crafting believable-sounding but totally fraudulent articles, typically for their own financial or political gain.

Because of the outsized influence of these fake news sites, especially during the 2016 presidential election, many view this sort of propaganda as a threat to democracy. If enough people believe the fake news, not only are voters misled but genuine news is delegitimized. It becomes more and more difficult for peo-ple to determine the real from the fake, and that shakes everything up.

Outright Lies

Not all of the untruths spread online come from organized fake news sites. Some of what you read on Facebook and other social media are plain old lies. You know, when someone deliberately says something that they know isn't true.

For some reason, some people have trouble calling a lie a lie. In the mainstream media, you're more likely to hear that someone "misspoke" or told an "untruth" or "falsehood." Sometimes a person is said to have "distorted the facts." And some politicians now refer to "alternative facts."

Whatever you call it, a lie is a lie, and the person telling it is a liar. But what if a person doesn't tell the original lie, they just pass it on via a social media post? The person sharing the lie has the excuse that someone else said it, and they're just relating it without judgment. This might technically absolve the second person from the original sin, but passing on a lie as if it's the truth is just as good as lying, if you ask me.

In any case, be on the lookout for people lying or sharing lies on Facebook and other social media. Again, just because someone (even someone important) says something doesn't make it true. It may not technically be fake news, but it's just as false.

Conspiracy Theories

Conspiracy theories have been around as long as anyone can remember; some people want to believe that certain events are much more complex than we are led to believe. There are people who believe that JFK's assassination was part of a nefarious plot, or that the moon landing was staged on a Hollywood set, or that Elvis Presley faked his own death. Despite facts proving otherwise, these conspiracy theories persist.

In fact, conspiracy theorists have become more emboldened in recent years, thanks to others sharing their theories over the Internet. Social media make it easier for those of like mind to pass their theories back and forth and to gain additional exposure to the previously uninitiated. If you haven't yet seen a particular conspiracy theory, it might look reasonable when you see it in a friend's news feed.

Social media have also helped spread newer conspiracy theories, often immediately after some tragic event in the news. More recent conspiracy theories have sprung up around climate change (it's a hoax perpetuated by greedy scientists), the 9/11 attacks (a "false flag" event planned by the U.S. government), vaccines and autism (the first causes the second), and Beyoncé (apparently she's been replaced by a clone). None of these theories has any amount of truth to them, yet they persist, especially in social media.

Why do some people believe these wild claims? For some, it's a way of trying to make sense out of seemingly random events. It just doesn't make any sense that a lone gunman could slip through the cracks and shoot a president, so there has to be more to the story. Hence the creation of a conspiracy behind the whole thing; that's somehow more comforting than acknowledging that random events sometimes just happen.

In any case, social media are rife with conspiracy theories of all shapes and sizes. Don't believe them.

Propaganda

Some of what people call fake news is actually propaganda—disinformation used to mislead or promote a particular point of view. Propaganda is particularly popular (and particularly potent) in politics, where one side spouts selective facts in an effort to promote its cause or disparage the opposite side.

We're all targets of propaganda—from one or the other political parties, from our government, even from foreign governments. For example, China has built a multi-billion dollar media empire to spread pro-Communist propaganda around the globe; Russia has similarly been accused of using propaganda to influence elections in several countries. And some claim that the Qatar-based Al Jazeera television network is being used to spread Islamic propaganda throughout the Middle East and beyond.

Political propaganda isn't new, nor is it limited to foreign actors. No doubt some people abroad see the broadcasts of Voice of America as a form of propaganda. For that matter, some conservatives in our country see certain news media as spreading left-wing propaganda—just as some liberals view other news media as spreading right-wing propaganda.

The fact is, big players—political parties, governments, and movements—have always used propaganda to influence the masses and will undoubtedly continue to do so. What's changed is they're now doing it via social media.

Biased News

Listen to some people in the political sphere, and you're bound to hear that this or that particular news outlet is "fake news." Although this can be the case, in most instances the person talking simply doesn't like the viewpoint espoused by that news outlet. That doesn't make the news from that outlet fake, but it could make it biased.

Let's be honest here. We live in a politically polarized society, where one side doesn't trust the other and few want to work together for the common good. This polarized environment spreads to news outlets big and small, with those of a particular viewpoint claiming that media with a different view are biased and not to be believed.

It is true that some news media strike a bias to the liberal or conservative side of things. For example, it's fair to say that Fox News is somewhat biased in a conservative direction, whereas MSNBC holds somewhat of a liberal bias. (Compared to these two outlets, most media observers find that CNN lies somewhere in the middle.) This can be seen by the stories they choose to cover, the "experts" they choose to interview, even the slant they put on their coverage. That doesn't mean their coverage is fraudulent, just that it comes from a certain viewpoint.

Ideally, you should know the political bias of a certain outlet and take that into account when reading something from it or watching it. I always think it's good if you can avoid getting all your news from outlets that share the same bias; you want to get a variety of viewpoints to avoid creating your own echo chamber.

>>>Go Further

FINDING RELIABLE MEDIA

How do you know if a given news source is reliable? One good test is if the outlet employs some sort of ombudsman to listen to consumer complaints and offer in-house criticism. If a newspaper or news channel is open to self-examination and free to issue corrections when they're wrong, you're in good hands.

AllSides (www.allsides.com), a site created to combat bias in the media, has rated the bias of more than 600 media outlets, and places the following in the center—meaning they're the least biased of all alternatives:

- Associated Press
- BBC
- Bloomberg
- Christian Science Monitor
- NPR (online news only)
- Reuters
- The Hill
- *USA Today*
- *The Wall Street Journal* (online news only)

Other well-known media show a slight bias to the left or right but still are fairly accurate in their reporting, compared to more biased outlets on the further extremes. So if you want to get the straight news with minimal bias and opinion, go to the major broadcast networks (ABC, CBS, NBC, and PBS), the major national newspapers and news magazines (*The New York Times, The New Yorker, USA Today, The Wall Street Journal, The Washington Post*), and legitimate online news sites (*Politico*, Yahoo! News). Also good are the Associated Press, CNN, and Reuters. Major foreign news sources, such as the BBC, *The Economist*, and *The Guardian*, are also relatively nonbiased.

Now, any and all of these media may print editorial pages or opinion pages, or offer their share of talking head interviews, all of which are ripe for biased opinion. But when it comes to straight news coverage, the mainstream media does a pretty good job.

Opinions

When I was a youngster, our household watched the *CBS Evening News* with Walter Cronkite. Mr. Cronkite spoke with an authority and engendered a level of trust not seen in today's generation of newsreaders. We watched CBS because we trusted Walter Cronkite.

Several days a week, at the end of the newscast, Walter turned the desk over to Eric Sevareid for two minutes of analysis and commentary. We knew this wasn't news reporting because the word *Commentary* appeared at the bottom of the screen. Mr. Sevareid was voicing his opinions, and they were clearly labeled as such. You could never question what his colleague Walter Cronkite said because it was hard news, but you were free to agree or disagree with Mr. Sevareid's opinions.

Fast-forward half a century and take a look at today's media landscape, where there are more opinions than facts being broadcast, whether on cable TV news networks or on talk radio. Much of the programming on MSNBC and Fox News is pure opinion, dominated by a coterie of talking heads and their slates of like-minded guests, and CNN isn't much better. Turn on the radio and all you hear are opinions. It's all talk, all the time, with very little news to break up the conversation.

There's nothing wrong with espousing one's opinion—over the airwaves or online—as long as it's clearly understood as such. The problem comes when viewers, listeners, or readers take these opinions as facts, and view the commentators as reporters. They're not. Sean Hannity and Rachel Maddow, as much as you might like or dislike them, are not journalists. They're commentators, offering their own opinions on the day's events. What they say may be interesting—and it might even be true—but it's always served up with that person's own particular brand of biases. It's not news, it's opinion—even if it's not always identified as such.

Fifty or so years ago, during the Cronkite/Sevareid era, television news belayed any potential confusion by clearly labeling the opinion pieces as *Commentary*. You couldn't easily confuse fact with opinion when that one word was emblazoned across the screen during the latter segments.

Today, however, opinions are seldom labeled or presented as such, especially online. Some people hear Hannity or Maddow and take their words as gospel—and share them on social media as such. That's not a good thing. Opinions are fine as long as we know they're just opinions. We cannot confuse them with facts.

So when you see someone quoting their favorite left- or right-wing commentator, know that you're hearing that person's opinion. The facts of the matter may be different.

Editorial Pages

The newspaper business approaches this situation by putting the opinions on the editorial pages. You know when you turn to the editorial pages you're not reading unbiased journalism; you're reading the opinions of the editorial staff. (This sometimes leads to a paper, such as *The Wall Street Journal*, having a fairly trusted and down-the-middle reputation for reporting while maintaining a reliably conservative editorial slant.)

Satire

Don't confuse fake news stories and websites with satirical articles and sites. Quite a few websites manufacture humorous stories in the name of entertainment, and it's easy to mistake some of these sites with honest-to-goodness news sites or their mirror-image fake news cousins.

Take, for example, The Onion (www.theonion.com). This site started out in 1988 as a satirical print newspaper, akin to *National Lampoon* and similar rags of the time, and it eventually made the transition to an online publication. It has an established reputation as a source of humorous made-up news stories, with headlines like "Winner Didn't Know It Was Pie-Eating Contest," "Drugs Win Drug War," "CIA Realizes It's Been Using Black Highlighters All These Years," and "People Far Away from You Not Actually Smaller."

Most of what The Onion publishes is quite silly and wouldn't be taken seriously by anyone paying attention. But there are other satirical sites out there that use actual events as the basis for their content, thus creating satirical stories that may be confusing to people reading them out of context.

In other words, not everybody gets the joke.

Here's an example from the parody news site The Daily Currant a few years back: The headline read "Sarah Palin to Join Al Jazeera as Host." The story was pretty funny but, as I said, not everybody got the joke. In this instance, the esteemed *Washington Post* got confused and cited this satirical story as fact in a profile of Palin. Whoops!

Other legitimate news organizations, both here and abroad, have been fooled by this type of satirical news item, as have millions of individuals who unwittingly repost the fake stories on Facebook and Twitter. I guess parody sounds all too real to some people, who then pass it on to their friends and family.

So satirical news stories aren't really fake news, but they're certainly not real news, either. They're meant to be funny and not to be taken seriously. If you run into one of these articles in your Facebook news feed and feel the urge to laugh, it's probably satire.

>>>*Go Further*

RUSSIA, FACEBOOK, AND THE 2016 PRESIDENTIAL ELECTION

If you read the (real) news, you're probably aware that Russia has been accused of extensive interference in the 2016 presidential election. This is real news, not fake: On February 16, 2018, Justice Department special counsel Robert Mueller indicted 13 Russian individuals and three companies of criminally conspiring to interfere with the 2016 U.S. presidential election. The charges allege that the Internet Research Agency (IRA), based in St. Petersburg, Russia, was the hub of online efforts to trick Americans into voting against Democratic candidate Hillary Clinton and for her Republican rival and eventual winner Donald Trump. These efforts involved the creation of fake news stories and propaganda, which were then disseminated across social media via the use of fake accounts and social media bots. (A bot is an automated fake account that fraudsters can use to create and spread fake news stories.)

The primary social medium used by the Russians was Facebook. They employed both human actors and automated bots to conduct what Deputy Attorney General Rod J. Rosenstein called "'information warfare against the United States with the stated goal of spread[ing] distrust towards the candidates and the political system in general." The Russian Internet trolls went to extensive means to make their posts look as if they were created by American citizens, relying on an 80-person team of graphics specialists, data analysts, and search engine optimization experts to create the false information.

Their efforts appeared in several forms on the Facebook site. The Russians created original posts intended to be shared by real users who shared the same political beliefs. They created fake user profiles and Facebook Pages, which they then used to share their fake posts and links. They also purchased advertisements on the Facebook site that pointed to similar fake stories on fake websites.

It's likely that you saw some of the Russian posts and ads, either directly or shared by some of your Facebook friends. And, if you clicked any of the Russian links, it's likely they collected your personal information (as stored on the Facebook site), which they then used to target you for further posts and fake news stories.

This is a big deal. A foreign country used Facebook to spread fake news and disinformation intended to influence the results of a U.S. presidential election. Facebook has faced much criticism in the wake of this situation and could face fines or stiffer regulation as punishment. In addition, there is every indication that Russia will attempt similar efforts in future campaigns—which means both Facebook and the government need to work on ways to prevent this kind of illegal foreign influence.

This is one of the downsides of social media, where innocent users are duped into doing the will of a foreign power. Undoubtedly Facebook will try to minimize the risk going forward, but it's ultimately your job to police your own News Feed and be on the lookout for fake news trying to influence your vote. The Russians are coming, and only you can guard against them.

Some "Fake News" Is Real

As if all the fictitious news stories floating about wasn't bad enough, the term *fake news* has been hijacked by politicians who use it to describe stories and news outlets that they dislike or disagree with. A politician may see a story that is particularly unflattering and call it "fake news" in an attempt to dismiss the story and the source as somehow illegitimate.

Of course, just because someone doesn't like a particular news story doesn't make the story "fake" or the facts incorrect. The reality is that most news items painted as "fake" by persons of power aren't fake at all. Even the most powerful people in the world can't make a genuine news story fake just by saying so—but they can smear that news source in the minds of their followers.

Attacking real news as "fake" is not only disingenuous, it's also dangerous. There are lots of facts that I don't happen to like, but I can't dispute them *because they are facts*. Facts are *not* opinions; they don't become less true just because you don't like what they mean.

So be wary of those who too quickly dismiss inconvenient truths as "fake news." You can't make bad news go away by questioning its validity. Facts are facts, even if you don't like them.

How to Tell Real News from Fake News

With all the fake news and outright lies circulating online, how do you distinguish the false facts from the real ones? After all, if you can't trust everything you see online (and you can't), then you have to do your homework to separate fact from fiction. No one else will do it for you.

Consider the Source

Whether you're dealing with Facebook or another social network, you should always consider where a piece of information came from. Some sources are more reliable than others—and some are obviously fake.

For example, if you see an article shared from CNN or ABC News or the AP, it's real news. If the article comes from a source that's less well-known, not known to you at all, or known to be a fake news site, you should treat that article with a grain of salt.

It's Not All Good

Check the URL

Be especially wary of fake news sites designed to look like legitimate news sites. You can often tell by a slight difference in their web URLs. For example, there's the legitimate CBS News site at www.cbsnews.com, and the fake site at www.cbsnews.com.co. That little extra ".co" at the end is a completely different web address that leads to a completely different—and completely fake—site.

Verify with Multiple Sources

If you're not sure about a given news article—either the article itself or the article's source—then see if you can find a similar story from another source you know is reliable. That means opening your web browser and doing an Internet search, or (if you're on Facebook) just searching from the Search box at the top of the news feed page.

If you can't find any corroborating stories, then it's likely the original story was fake. If you do find similar stories, but they're all from similarly questionable sources, then the original story might still be fake. If, on the other hand, you find similar stories from trusted sources, then the story is probably okay.

Consider What Is Being Said

Sometimes the best way to tell whether a story is fake is to simply trust your nose. If it smells fake, it probably is.

For example, would you believe a story with the headline "President Trump to Give All Legal Voters $1000"? Although this would be nice if true, it just doesn't seem likely. It smells funny, and it is funny, too.

This doesn't always go the other direction, however. Some fake news is designed to sound legitimate, even if it isn't. A headline like "Firefighter Jailed 30 Days by Atheist Mayor for Praying at Scene of Fire" isn't wildly outlandish, and it might even sound like something that could happen. It might pass your smell test, even though it's fake from start to finish.

All in all, though, trust your instincts. If something doesn't seem plausible, dig into it a little more to evaluate the source and legitimacy of the article. Don't accept questionable content at face value.

Check with Snopes

When I'm not sure whether something is fake or real, I consult a site that specializes in debunking fake news and urban legends. Snopes (www.snopes.com) is a reliable source for debunking falsehoods or confirming truthful information you find on the Internet. It's original and primary focus is on urban legends, but it's become a fact-checking site for all sorts of fake (and real) news articles.

You can browse the latest and most popular news articles and urban legends, or use the top-of-page search box to search for specific news items in which you're interested. Just enter the title of the questionable article and Snopes likely has information about it. Snopes tells you if a given article is true, false, or some-where in between.

Check with Media Bias/Fact Check

The Media Bias/Fact Check website (www.mediabiasfactcheck.com) lists most known major media outlets, and assigns them a place on a sliding left-to-right scale, in terms of bias. You can enter the name of a particular news website or organization and find out whether it has a leftward bias, a right-leaning bias, or is relatively unbiased. You also can find out a given site's conspiracy level (Mild to Tin Foil Hat) and pseudo-science level (Mild to Quackery). It's a great way to see how legitimate a site is, as well as how biased it may be.

If a Politician Says It's Fake, It's Probably Real

Finally, remember that some politicians like to label negative news stories they don't like as "fake news," even though it isn't. So if a senator or congressperson or even the president himself labels a story as fake news, it's probably real news. Don't fall for their misdirection!

>>>*Go Further*

FIGHTING FAKE NEWS ON FACEBOOK

Facebook is far and away the most used social medium today. Unfortunately, Facebook has also been the most common vehicle for fake news and misleading information due to users sharing inaccurate posts with their friends on the site.

Facebook realizes this and is trying various approaches to identify or remove obvious fake posts and propaganda. Initially, Facebook tried to "flag" fake news stories on its site but found that putting a red flag on a story actually encouraged people to read it. (That's called an *unintended consequence*.)

Today, Facebook tries to fight fake news at the source, by identifying false or misleading posts and removing them. This is an arduous job and not always accurate; sometimes Facebook misses obvious fake posts and sometimes the company removes real posts instead. It's not perfect, but they're trying.

To assist in these efforts, Facebook lets you report posts that you think contain false information. Tap or click the More (three dots) button in the top-right corner of a post and then select Give Feedback on This Post. When the next panel appears, select False News (or any other appropriate reason) and then click or tap Send. Facebook uses your feedback to look at and determine what to do with this post.

By the way, if you're seeing a lot of fake posts from one particular person, you also can use this process to unfollow this user. If you're getting inundated with questionable posts from a given person, this may be the best course of action.

How to Avoid Spreading Fake News

Hopefully the information in this chapter has alerted you to the problem of fake news and fraudulent information you might find on Facebook and other social media. You've learned what fake news is and how to identify it.

Your challenge from here is not only to avoid being influenced by fake news but also not to spread it to your friends and family. To be a responsible social media user, you need to keep your news feed as factual as possible and avoid spreading information of questionable validity.

Here's what you need to do.

Read It Before You Share It

Believe it or not, the majority of people who share stories via Facebook don't actually read those stories all the way to the end before they post. A lot of folks read only the headline and post it without reading anything. That's irresponsible.

If you're going to share something with people you know and respect, respect them enough to read the thing you're sharing. You might discover, on closer inspection, that the article is obviously fraudulent, that it doesn't actually say what the headline promises, or that you disagree with what it ends up saying. If you want your friends to read it, the least you can do is read it first.

Check It Out Before You Share It

Don't share things that you suspect are fake. Use all the techniques you've learned in this chapter, including the Snopes and Media Bias/Fact Check web-sites, to check the validity of the article; don't just blindly repost things you see in your news feed. Make sure it's factual before you share it.

If Someone Questions It, Remove It

If you somehow end up posting something that isn't factual, and someone points out to you that that's the case, go back and delete. Facebook, Twitter, and other social media let you remove your posts after you've posted; you should do this if you discover you've posted some fake news. It's a way of correcting your mis-takes, and you need to do this. (You may even want to create a new post reveal-ing the new information you have about the first post, to completely clear the air.)

Bottom line, you need to be careful about what you share on social media. There's a lot of phony stuff out there, and you don't want to be duped into shar-ing it with people who trust you. Keep their trust by not posting fake news.

This Week in Fake News

Want to keep up with the latest real news about fake news? Then check out my companion blog, This Week in Fake News (twifn.home.blog). Every Friday I update readers on the fake news headlines from the previous week. There's always enough to fill up an entire blog post!

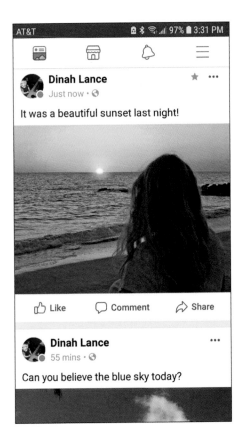

In this chapter, you discover the best ways to post on social media and find out what you should and shouldn't post.

- → Writing a Proper Post
- → Posting Things That People Want to Read
- → Things You Probably *Shouldn't* Share Online
- → Ten Things to Avoid When Posting Online
- → Joining a Conversation—or Not

3

What to Share—and What *Not* to Share—on Social Media

Using social media is all about being social and sharing your thoughts, experiences, photos, and more. That said, is everything you do and think ripe for sharing? What do your online friends want to see—and what would they rather *not* see from you?

Deciding what to share on social media is a delicate dance. Share too much (or the wrong things) and your friends will quit reading your posts and maybe even "unfriend" you. Share too little and your friends will forget you're even there. You need to figure out just what kinds of things to share and how often to share them.

Writing a Proper Post

When it comes to posting something on social media, *how* you post is often as important as *what* you post. There's a right way to post your messages, and many wrong ways to do so.

Messages, Posts, and Status Updates

Don't get confused by the nomenclature. What you call a message probably goes by a different name on different social networks. Some call messages *posts*, others call them *status updates*. On Twitter, the messages you post are called *tweets*. The format might be different, but they're all just different names for the same thing—the thoughts and information you share with others online.

Keep It Short

A short post — I am digging this groovy weather!

Anything you post to Facebook or Twitter or most other social media should be concise and to the point. Even though most social media accept posts as long as you like (Twitter, which has a 280-character limit, being the exception), that doesn't mean that you *should* ramble on for multiple paragraphs. Most people don't really read the posts in their news feeds; instead, they skim through them, kind of like reading headlines in a newspaper.

News Feed

A *news feed* (on some networks simply called a *feed*) displays a stream of posts or status updates from your friends or contacts on that social network.

You see, a social media post is not a blog post or an entry in your diary; it's more like an item in a news ticker. Put another way, a social media post is a news bulletin, not a feature story. So say what you need to say and be done with it.

This means you should try to keep your posts to no more than a few sentences. Just long enough to get your point across, but not so long that readers will get bored. If your posts are too long, your friends will simply skip over them. Shorter is sweeter.

When you don't have the space to provide a lot of background information in a particular post, you can also link to more information. If there's more behind the story, include a link to a web page that offers more details. Readers can click the link to read more on the linked-to site.

Keep It Casual

Acronyms ——

Sentence fragment

In your goal of creating short but memorable posts, know that you can take some grammatical shortcuts. Unlike formal letter or email writing, when posting to social media, you don't have to use full sentences or proper grammar. In fact, it's okay to use common abbreviations and acronyms, such as BTW (by the way) and LOL (laughing out loud).

To that end, your writing style should be casual, not formal. Write like you speak. Imagine yourself sitting with a group of friends in your local bar or coffee shop, telling them the latest piece of information. Whatever you would say to them is what you should write in your post. Avoid unnecessary formality; casual is good.

That doesn't mean you can get sloppy. Although you don't have to use complete, proper grammar and punctuation, you want to avoid unnecessary misspellings. Misspelled words mark you as less informed than you might actually be and cause people to take you less seriously. Take the time to spell things correctly.

A post in all caps—AVOID

Also, and this is important, although you don't have to use 100% totally correct grammar and punctuation, you should never write in all capital letters. WHEN YOU WRITE IN ALL CAPS, IT LOOKS LIKE YOU'RE YELLING. Learn how to use the Shift key and *not* the Caps Lock key on your keyboard. You don't have to properly capitalize every word (especially if you're typing on your smartphone), but don't capitalize every word and every letter. Just don't.

Show It If You Can

A post accompanied by a photograph

The world around us is becoming more visual. To that end, more and more social media posts include images, either as the sole content of the post or to supplement an accompanying text message. Pictures are important.

Let's face it, when reading onscreen, your eyes are drawn to any pictures on the page. We like looking at pictures, especially pictures of people. If you have a picture in your post, more people will look at it than if the post were text-only. If you want to draw attention to a post, include a picture. It's that simple.

In fact, some social media are built around image sharing. Pinterest and Instagram, for example, are visual social networks. Yes, you can add descriptions to your Pinterest pins and Instagram photos, but it's really the images that you're sharing on these services.

You can include images with your posts to most other social media, too. Even Twitter, which originally allowed only text messages, now lets you include photos with your tweets. My Facebook News Feed is almost exclusively composed of status updates with photos. Like I said, we live in a visual world—and we need to communicate visually.

This might mean that you upload a photo to accompany the text message you planned to post. It might mean you post only a photo that you've taken with your smartphone or previously stored on your computer. If social media help you document your life, an important part of that documentation will be in the form of digital photographs.

You're not limited to photos, though. Most social media let you post videos along with your text-based messages. The video is probably something you shot with your smartphone or tablet—or even (with some social networks) live video of what you're doing at this moment. If pictures are good, moving pictures are better!

>>>*Go Further*

HOW OFTEN SHOULD YOU POST?

One of the most common questions I get concerns frequency. When it comes to sharing on social media, just how often should you post?

The general answer to this question is that you should post frequently—but not too frequently. Social media create communities, and to be a member of any such community, you have to actively participate. You aren't required to post anything to social media, but if you wait too long between posts, people will forget that you're there. You have to be somewhat active, or you might as well not be there at all.

Conversely, if you post too frequently, people might perceive your posts as overbearing or annoying. You can overpost and wear out your welcome. If you have too many pointless posts clogging your friends' feeds, they'll block your posts. Nobody likes a conversation hog, either online or in the real world. Don't bombard your friends with too much information.

As to specific recommendations, that differs from site to site. When it comes to Facebook, the best frequency is somewhere between once a week and a few times per day. Younger users tend to expect more frequent postings, but for us grown-ups, once every day or two is probably good.

If we're talking about Twitter, those users expect more frequent postings—up to several times a day. Pinterest users are comfortable with a few pins a day, often done in batches. And LinkedIn's business/professional focus argues for fewer postings, once or twice a week, tops.

Probably the best way to judge how often to post is to examine the posts in your own news feed. Look at those friends whose posts you look forward to rather than those you get tired of reading. The person who leaves you asking for more probably has the frequency right.

Posting Things That People Want to Read

When you use social media, it's easy to think that it's all about *you*. It's you writing your posts, after all, discussing things that happened to you and are of interest to you. It's your life you're sharing!

Except that it really isn't. Yes, you are posting things about you, but you want your friends to read those things and interact with you about them. If you're selfish about what you post, your friends will tune you out and you'll only be talking to yourself. As with any social situation, you want to initiate a conversation—and that means keeping your audience in mind when you post.

In other words, you need to post about things that are of interest to your friends. If a post is only of interest to you, no one else will read it.

News Updates

One very important use of social media is to keep your family and friends up to date on your latest personal news. One post can inform a large number of people about something important; it's a lot more efficient than sending out dozens of emails or making tons of phone calls.

Important information in a post ⟶

What, then, counts as interesting information that your friends will want to read? Here are some suggestions:

- Post things that are important to you and your friends. We're talking moments and events that are important to *you*, but that you also think your *friends* might care about, too.

- Post things that your friends and family want to know about. Friends typically want to know if you've done or seen something interesting, taken a vacation, met a mutual friend, and such. If you think someone's interested in it, post it.

- Post about major life events—things in your life that your friends and family *need* to know about. These are important moments and events, such as anniversaries, birthdays, graduations, celebrations, and the like.

- Post important news updates. If you have recently been ill or hospitalized, update your friends on how you're doing. If you have a new job or a new volunteer position, let your friends know. If you've moved to a new house or condo, spread the word via a social media post. If something important has happened in your life, update friends and family via social media.

- Post important news about your spouse or partner. Your social media updates don't always have to be about you. Many of your friends are likely mutual friends of your spouse, so if anything major has happened to your partner, include that information in your status update—especially if she can't post herself, for whatever reason.

- Post important news about other family members (with their permission, of course). You might know something about a cousin or nephew that others in your family might not have yet heard. Share your information with other family members via a social media post.

- Post about mutual friends. It's tough to keep track of all your old friends. Start the chain by posting what you know, and let your other friends pass it on to their friends, too.

- Post about upcoming events. If there's something coming up that's important to you and interesting to your friends, let them know. Maybe you're singing at an upcoming concert or worship service, maybe you have a big golf tournament, maybe you're hosting or participating in a big charity event. If you want your friends to know about (and maybe attend) the event, then post about it.

- Post interesting thoughts. Look, you've come this far in life; you've earned your opinions. Share your wisdom with your friends and family via Facebook status updates—in a noncontroversial, inoffensive way, if you can.

- Post links to news stories your friends will find interesting. Many people get their news from social media, primarily from friends who share articles of interest. Don't overdo it, and know your audience, but it's okay to socially share the news of the day.

It's Not All Good

Is It Really Interesting?

Just because something is interesting to you doesn't mean it's interesting to anyone else. The fact that you went to a concert or read a good book is interesting; that you woke up with a headache or just had a cup of tea is not. I've seen too many posts of things my friends find "cute" (cats, in particular) that I could not care less about. Try to look at things from someone else's perspective before you post.

Things You Probably *Shouldn't* Share Online

With all the interesting bits of information you can and should share via social media, there are also lots of things you probably shouldn't.

Social networks are meant to be social; they want your posts to be seen by as many people as possible. This isn't private email we're talking about. Social networks are *public* networks, not private ones.

Because everything is so public, you can do a lot of damage to yourself by posting something stupid. And people post stupid, harmful stuff all the time. It's like some folks forget that social media are public media, not private media. Just remember, everything you post can and probably will become public—and ultimately come back to haunt you.

What and how much personal information to share via Facebook and other social media depends to a degree on your personal comfort level and your personal life. But in general, you shouldn't share any information that might prove embarrassing to you or your family, or that might compromise your current job or associations, or future job prospects. (Or, for that matter, that might make you vulnerable to identity theft.)

Naturally, what all this means is going to differ from person to person. If you serve on a homeowner's association filled with ultra-conservative neighbors, for example, you might not want to give them constant reminders that you're a dyed-in-the-wool liberal. And if all your golfing buddies are agnostics, you might not want to make a big deal about being a born-again Christian.

But it goes further than that. If you're preaching the "just say no" drug message to your children or grandchildren, you might not want to list *Cheech & Chong's Up in*

Smoke as one of your favorite movies; it might compromise your integrity on the matter just a bit. For that matter, you might want to hide all those photos that show you drinking margaritas on the beach, for both your kids' sake and to ward off any awkward questions from teetotalling employers or neighbors.

In fact, pictures can be more damaging than words. A picture of you holding a cigarette in your hand could be used by your insurance company to raise your health insurance rates. Photos of you partying hearty or just acting goofy can raise doubts about your decision-making abilities. Do you really want your pastor or your grandkids or your ex-husband's lawyer to see you in compromising positions?

The same goes with the content you post on social media sites. There are stories, some of them true, of careless (and carefree) employees posting about this afternoon's golf game when they were supposed to be home sick from work. Employers (and spouses and just about anyone else) can and will keep track of you online, if you're stupid enough to post all your comings and goings.

And it's not just factual stuff. Spouting off your opinions is a common-enough online activity, but some people will disagree with you or take more serious offense. Do you really want to get into an online argument over something you posted in haste after a few drinks at the club? In this age of increasingly polarized politics, know that if you go off on an anti-liberal or anti-conservative rant, you're going to offend somebody. It's okay to vent your opinions, but be prepared to deal with the social consequences.

For that matter, it's a really bad idea to use social media to criticize the people you work for, the people you work with, or the people you associate with in the community. Posting about how much you hate the president of the neighborhood association will eventually get back to her, and then you have a whole bunch of fences to mend.

The Golden Rule

When posting to social media, follow the online golden rule: Post only about others as you would have them post about you. If you can't say something nice, don't say anything at all.

With some social media, such as Facebook, you have the option of making a given post visible only to those on your friends list. Although it might be tempting to share intimate details with your online friends, think about who these "friends" really are. How many of your social media friends are close, intimate friends? How many are merely acquaintances, or just people you work with or went to school with? How many are people you really don't know at all?

If you have a hundred or so people on your friends list, that's a hundred or so people who could be reading about how you hate your kids, or how you cheated the IRS, or how you really feel about the people you work with. It's not hard to imagine how this personal information can come back to haunt you.

What you have to remember is that on social media, you're not invisible. It's a public community; everything you post may be readable by anyone. Post only that information that would be safe enough for your family, friends, and co-workers to read.

You see, on social media, discretion is definitely the better part of valor. When in doubt, don't post it. It's okay to keep some thoughts to yourself; you don't have to post every little thing you think or that happens to you.

It's Not All Good

How Do Others Do It?

If you're not sure whether or how to post something on social media, you don't have to reinvent any wheels. Chances are someone else has faced the same dilemma and discovered the right (or wrong) way to deal with this situation.

To this end, one of the best ways to learn proper social media etiquette is to observe how others do it. Observe how and what your friends post (especially those you find particularly engaging), and mimic their behavior. If it works for them, it'll probably work for you, too. As I said, there's no reason to reinvent the wheel; learn from the people who came before you.

Ten Things to Avoid When Posting Online

With the previous advice in mind, here are ten things you probably shouldn't do when posting to social media.

1. Don't Post if You Don't Have Anything to Say

Some of the most annoying people on Facebook, Twitter, and other social media are those who post their every action and movement. ("I just woke up." "I'm reading my mail." "I'm thinking about having lunch." "That coffee was delicious.") Post if there's something interesting happening, but avoid posting just to be posting. Think about what you like to read about other people, and post in a similar fashion.

2. Don't Pick a Fight

Many people use social media as a platform for their opinions. While it may be okay to share your opinions with close (that is, real-world) friends, spouting off in a public forum is not only bad form, it's a way to incite a *flame war*—an unnecessary online war of words.

So don't deliberately post controversial opinions just to stir the pot—and don't feel compelled to add your (conflicting) opinions as comments on other posts. Social media are not the places to argue politics, religion, or other sensitive subjects. Save your inflammatory comments for your family's Thanksgiving dinner.

3. Don't Post Anything That Could Be Used Against You

Want to put your job in jeopardy? Then by all means, you should post negative comments about your workplace or employer. Want your partner to walk out on you? Then share your petty personal beefs with the entire online world. You get the picture; anything you post online can and probably will be used against you. So don't post negative personal comments or attacks that are better kept private. If you're in doubt, don't post it; it's better to be safe than sorry.

4. Don't Post Overly Personal Information

Along the same lines, think twice before sharing the intimate details of your private life—including embarrassing photographs. Discretion is a value we older folks should maintain; there's no reason for posting pictures of you falling down drunk at the holiday office party or baring it all on the beach during your last vacation. Leave some of the details to imagination.

Similarly, not everyone wants to hear the gory details of your latest knee surgery, what you found in your teenaged son's room yesterday, or what color underwear you're wearing—or if you're not wearing underwear at all. There's the concept of TMI (too much information), and you want to avoid including TMI in your social media posts. If you'd rather not see those kinds of details about other people, don't subject them to your similar details, either. There's such a thing as oversharing.

5. Don't Gripe

Building on that last tip, the last thing I (and lots of others) want to find in our news feeds are your private gripes. We really, really don't care if your husband leaves the toilet seat up or if your next-door neighbor hasn't mowed his lawn in two weeks. Oh, it's okay to grouse and be grumpy from time to time, but don't use social media as your personal forum for petty grievances. If you have a personal problem, deal with it. You don't have to share *everything*, you know. Whining gets old really fast.

This is especially the case when you're complaining about the people you work with or deal with on a daily basis. Yeah, I know, your boss (or the leader of the neighborhood commission) is a jerk, but it's nothing I can do anything about. On the other hand, if this jerk sees your posts, you've just created a bit of an awkward situation for yourself. Remember, social media are public media, and if you post it, your boss or group leader or whomever will eventually see it (especially if troublemaking co-workers point it out to him). Don't post anything that you don't want someone to see. Period.

6. Don't Post Personal Contact Information

As nice as Facebook and other social media are for renewing old acquaintances, they also can put you in contact with people you really don't want to be in contact with. So don't make it easy for disreputable people or unwanted old boyfriends to find you offline; avoid posting your phone number, email address, and home address.

Posting this sort of information also can put you at risk for identity theft. Avoid posting anything that a digital thief could use to gain access to your personal accounts. That means not only your address, phone number, and such, but also information that could be used to guess your passwords—your mother's maiden name, your birthdate, your pet's name, your favorite color, and so forth. And definitely never, ever post your Social Security number.

A large part of keeping yourself safe online is simply not doing anything dumb. Posting personal information on social media is dumb. So don't do it.

7. Don't Post Your Constant Whereabouts

For that matter, you don't need to broadcast your every movement; thieves don't need to know when you're away from home. When you post that you're having a wonderful dinner downtown, or enjoying your week-long vacation in Florida, you're advertising to anyone and everyone that your house is empty and ripe for the picking. You don't need to give the bad guys such a blatant heads up.

Similarly, you don't want people you don't like to know where you are right now. If someone is out to get you, they don't need to know that you're enjoying cocktails at the corner of Fifth and Main. You want to minimize contact with unfriendly people, not make it easier for them to harass you.

In short, it's okay to post where you were *after the fact*, but not beforehand. You want to keep your current whereabouts private.

Similarly, don't post information about your daily or weekly routines. You don't want to tell the bad guys that you're always in yoga class on Wednesdays at 4:00, or have a standing golf game every Saturday morning at the club. Keep your routines private.

8. Don't Post Rumors, Hoaxes, and Urban Legends

As you learned in Chapter 2, "Separating Fact from Fiction Online," social media are rife with rumors, half-truths, and misinformation. Did you hear the one about the sick child who's collecting get well cards or needs you to "like" or share his post? Or the one about the government secretly plotting martial law? Or the "advice" that entering your PIN in reverse at an ATM will summon the police? Or that Macaulay Culkin (or Bill Nye or Will Smith or some other well-known celebrity) has died—in spite of his protests to the contrary?

These posts are all false. They spread lies and untruths, and take up valuable bandwidth in your news feed. Some people obviously believe them; others see them for what they are—urban legends, conspiracy theories, and "fake news" that mislead the gullible among us.

Unfortunately, these questionable posts are often quite popular, going viral as they're shared from one person to another. In the old days, your crazy relatives shared these sorts of posts via email; today, people share them via Facebook and Twitter. If you've been on social media at all, you've no doubt seen your share of them.

These posts are easily identified as what they are, which is total cow manure. You should never, ever share or retweet these sorts of posts. You should never start new ones yourself, unless it's very clearly a joke. A lot of people believe these things, and we don't need to contribute to their lack of intelligence. Just ignore them.

9. Don't Post About People Without Their Permission

Social networks are great for sharing things that you do. But you shouldn't use social media to post too much about other people without their permission. It's okay to let your friends know what other mutual friends are up to, but you can't speak for those other people. Posting information that's publicly known is one thing, but sharing personal secrets is quite another.

Similarly, you shouldn't post pictures of other people without first getting their permission—especially if those pictures are in any way compromising. Even though *you* may be okay with it, a lot of people don't want their mugs plastered all over Facebook or Instagram. Some people want to remain more private, and we need to respect their wishes.

Now, this can be a tricky issue. What if you're taking pictures at a neighborhood block party—are those pictures of your neighbors okay to post? What about pictures you took at your son's graduation or your granddaughter's birthday party? These are all public events, and thus might be fair game—until you run into that one neighbor or parent who doesn't want her pictures or her children's pictures posted publicly. Like I said, it's tricky.

The best approach is to ask permission before you post. Most people will say okay. If you can't ask permission, don't post that particular photo of or information about that person. Or you can go ahead and post it but take it down if someone complains. I recommend the more discreet approach, but I do admit that I've posted without permission on occasion.

Some venues will ask that you don't post pictures of their events. In this instance, respect the request. I recently attended my grandson's preschool graduation ceremony, and the teachers explicitly asked that group pictures not be posted to Facebook or other social media because some parents don't want their children thus exposed. That was a fair request, and one I honored. You should do the same in similar situations.

Finally, consider which pictures of your kids and grandkids are appropriate to post. That picture of your granddaughter in her swim suit may be cute to you but lascivious to someone else—and potentially embarrassing to her. We all want to show off our kids and grandkids, and I'm the worst offender in this, but sometimes family pictures should be limited to family only.

10. Don't Post Sensitive Information

Finally, if your work or social activities involve sensitive or confidential information, for goodness sakes, don't spill that information online. Avoid posting about the project you're working on, or even that you're working on a project. Don't share details that competitors or opponents might find useful. Don't violate any confidentiality agreements, and don't abuse your employer's trust. Social media are great for sharing what you do on your personal time, but not at all appropriate for sharing what you do during work hours. Leave it at work; don't share it on Facebook.

Joining a Conversation—or Not

Given the social nature of social media, you're encouraged to comment on other people's posts, to join in the conversation, and to share what you read with others. But should you always jump in the middle of an online conversation? And are there posts you see that you shouldn't share?

When to Join a Conversation, and When to Bow Out

Commenting on another person's post

Social networks and online message boards let you comment on the posts that others make, and in the process, create ongoing conversations. You comment on a post, someone comments on your comment, you respond to that, and on it goes. It's part of what makes social media so social.

Most social media conversations are good. Some aren't. Some devolve into online shouting matches. Others just get silly. Still others would be better served as a private chat between two people, not as a public message thread.

When, then, should you join the conversation? And when should you exercise more restraint and not add your two cents' worth?

Here are some do's and don'ts for joining conversations in social media:

- **Do** join a conversation when input is asked for or encouraged.
- **Don't** join a conversation if your input is no more substantive than "Me too" or "You bet."
- **Do** join a conversation if you have knowledge or experience that would be useful or interesting.
- **Don't** join a conversation if you have absolutely nothing new or unique to add—or if you simply don't know what you're talking about.
- **Do** join a conversation to lend support to a friend. Sometimes a comment can be like a virtual hug or pat on the back, and that's a good thing.
- **Don't** join a conversation just to cause trouble. We're talking randomly negative comments that have little bearing on the original post, save to raise the hackles of those reading. This is commonly called *trolling*, and you shouldn't do it. If it's obvious that you're among a group of right-wing Republicans,

there's not a whole lot of good that can come out of posting your left-wing Democratic opinions; you're not going to convert anybody—you're just going to make them mad at you. As tempting as it might be to sound off against those you disagree with, there's really no point in being a troublemaker.

- **Do** join a conversation if you can move it forward, by providing additional information or viewpoints.

- **Don't** join a conversation just to hijack it in a different direction. It's not your conversation; it belongs to the person who started it. Keep things on track!

In short, an online conversation is just like one in the real world. If you can add something to the mix without derailing it, then join in. If you have nothing important to add, then don't.

What to Share—and What *Not* to Share

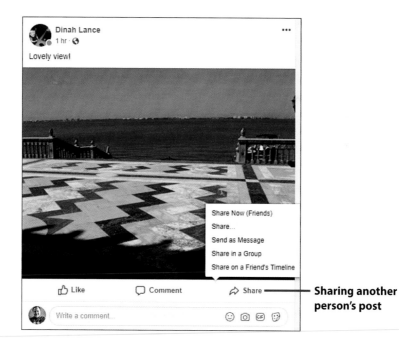

Sharing another person's post

Sometimes you run into a post from someone that you think your friends might find interesting. Maybe it's a link to an informative web page. Maybe it's a cute photograph. Maybe it's just some interesting information. Facebook and other social media let you share these posts with your online friends. (Twitter calls this *retweeting*.)

The problem is, if you share too many things on your news feed, people are going to start tuning out. You want them to see the interesting things you share, which is difficult if you're clogging the feed with too many uninteresting or irrelevant things you've shared.

The key, as with all posting, is to know what your friends will find interesting and what they'll find frivolous. Here are some tips:

- **Do** share items of direct interest to your online friends.

- **Don't** share items that you find interesting but your friends won't.

- **Do** share items your friends are likely not to have seen otherwise.

- **Don't** share items that you've seen repeatedly online. Chances are that your friends have already seen it, too.

- **Do** share funny pictures and videos. If they made you laugh, they'll probably amuse your friends, too. (But exercise some restraint; no one really wants to see the twentieth cat video you posted today.)

- **Don't** share items that you haven't independently verified. The last thing you want to do is spread inaccurate information, fake news, or urban legends—or even URLs that lead nowhere. (And don't assume that just because you saw it online or on TV or in another person's feed that an item is true; fake news is often more visible these days than real news!)

- **Do** share posts from friends and family members, if they're relevant.

- **Don't** share photos of people who don't want their pictures shared. For that matter, don't share any private information that you have in your possession.

- **Do** share pictures of your younger children and grandchildren. People like looking at cute family pictures—as long as you don't overdo it. (And as long as the pictures aren't inappropriate, of course.)

- **Don't** share inflammatory messages, photos, and hate speech. If you can't be civil and respect others' opinions and rights, you don't belong on social media.

When to Tag Yourself—and Others—in Photos

Tagging another person in a photo

Then there's the issue of *tagging*, identifying yourself or someone else in a picture that's been posted online. Facebook and other social media let you tag people in photos; in fact, many people tag themselves and their friends when they post their pictures. You can also jump in after the fact and tag people you know (yourself included) when viewing others' photos.

At first blush, identifying people in a picture sounds like a good thing, like you're helping out the person who posted that photo and didn't add any tags. Maybe you know someone in the photo he didn't, after all.

The problem is that not everyone wants to be singled out online. Tagging a person has the unfortunate effect of making that photo visible to all of that person's friends, even if she doesn't want her friends to see it. Maybe the photo is less than flattering, or records embarrassing or unwise behavior, or places that person in a place where he doesn't want people to see him. In essence, tagging a person without his knowledge or permission can cause all sorts of problems for the person being tagged, even if it's just giving that person a little more visibility than he might want.

The bottom line on this one is pretty clear. Unless you know the person wants to be tagged, you shouldn't tag him. Maybe that means asking first, maybe it means not tagging that person in the photo, maybe it means not posting the photo at all. Some people like to remain as anonymous as possible; you should respect that decision and err on the side of caution.

4

Using Social Media—Safely and Privately

How safe are social media? If you use social media, is your personal information at risk? Can you be harmed using social media?

The reality is that social media are as safe, or as risky, as anything on the Internet. If you use social media intelligently and responsibly, you can minimize whatever risks exist.

Is It Safe to Use Social Media?

There are potential hazards involved in virtually every online activity, from reading emails to web browsing. Such hazards also exist with the use of social media, such as Facebook.

What kinds of hazards are we talking about? There are both major and minor ones, including the following:

- **Viruses and other malware:** Like any website, posts on a social networking site can contain links to viruses, spyware, and other forms of malicious software (malware), on either your computer or mobile device. If you click or tap on a bad link, often disguised as a link to an interesting website or app, you can infect your device with this type of malicious software.

Malware

A *virus* is a malicious software program that can cause damage to an infected computer, smartphone, or tablet. *Spyware* is a similar but different software program that obtains information from your device without your knowledge or consent. Both viruses and spyware are forms of malicious software—*malware* for short.

- **Spam:** Users who publicly post their email addresses on Facebook and other social media can find themselves the target of unwanted junk email, or spam. Spammers harvest email addresses from social networking sites and add these addresses to their email mailing lists for sending spam messages.

- **Identity theft:** Posting personal information publicly on Facebook and similar social media can result in *identity theft*. Identity thieves use this public information to assume a user's identity on the social network or on other websites; to apply for credit cards and loans in the user's name; to legitimize undocumented foreign workers; and to gain access to the user's banking and credit card accounts.

Identity Theft

Identity theft is a form of fraud in which one person pretends to be someone else, typically by stealing personal information, such as a bank number, credit card number, or Social Security number. The intent of identity theft is often to steal money or obtain other benefits.

- **Violation of your privacy:** It's not just the information you post publicly that's at risk. The big social media companies base their business models on being able to sell to other companies (advertisers, primarily) not only the information you willingly provide but also information about what you read and do on their sites. Everything you do on Facebook, Twitter, and their ilk is tracked and sold and used to try to sell you stuff and influence your future behavior.

- **Cyberbullying:** It's unfortunate, but many people employ social media to bully people they dislike. This is particularly common among school-age users, but it can happen to people of any age. Some online bullies post threatening messages on their victims' profile pages; others go to the extreme of creating fake profile pages for their victims, full of embarrassing fictitious information. Cyberbullying is particularly troublesome, as it can be completely anonymous but have the same debilitating effects as physical bullying.

- **Online stalking:** Online stalkers like to follow their victims from one website or social network to another. If granted friend status, these online bullies—often pretending to be someone that they're not—will try to become close to you, whether for their own personal enjoyment or to cause you discomfort, embarrassment, or actual harm.

- **Physical stalking or harassment:** Some online predators take their stalking into the physical world. This is facilitated when you post personal information—including phone numbers and home addresses—on Facebook and other social networking sites. This information helps predators physically contact their victims, which can result in harassment or even physical violence.

- **Robbery:** Have you ever posted on Facebook about going out for dinner on a given evening, or about getting ready to take a long vacation? When you do so, you're telling potential robbers when your home will be empty—and that your belongings are ripe for the taking.

Scary stuff, all of it.

That said, there are steps you can take to make social media safer. If you post a plethora of personal information, you'll be less safe than if you are more discreet. If you avoid posting personal details about your life, you'll be safer from potential attackers or identity thieves than if you post liberally about your activities.

How do you avoid these potential dangers? Well, the only sure way to be completely safe is to delete all your profiles and cease using Facebook and other social media. Short of that, however, you can network in relative safety by being smart about what you post and what you respond to on the site.

Smarter Social Networking

I can give you lots of advice on how to keep safe on social media. (And I will, I promise!) But all the tips I can supply boil down to this: You have to use your head. Safe social networking is smart social networking. While various social media have various privacy and security tools you can employ, nothing will keep you safer than thinking before you click. The riskiest behavior comes from not considering all the consequences of what you might do. The safest users are those that don't do dumb things. So don't do dumb things.

Repeat: Don't do dumb things.

Now, to the more detailed recommendations—all of which involve smarter social networking.

Think Before You Click or Tap

You'll see lots of posts in your news feeds with clickable links—to other websites, to online articles, to photos and videos on other sites, you name it. Not every link is what it seems to be, however.

Just as with email, many disreputable types like to "phish" for information by posting links that look to be one thing but are actually something quite different. A link might purport to take you to an interesting news story, but in fact drop you on a page full of annoying advertisements. Or it might look like an official Facebook or Twitter link, but instead lead to a phony (but official-looking) web page that tries to get you to enter your username and password, while tricking you into revealing your personal information.

The reality is, there are a lot of links in social media that are something less than what they seem. Most of these deceptive links (sometimes called *clickbait*) merely lead to advertising-laden pages (so-called *click farms*, because the owner gets paid whenever someone clicks on an ad). But others are more dangerous in the way they phish for personal information.

So take care before you click or tap any link you find in your social network news feed. That's true even if the link is in a post from a trusted friend; even trusted friends can be deceived. And after you click, be ready to hit the back button if what you see isn't what you expect.

Think Before You Post

Just as you need to be smart about what you click in friends' posts, you also need to be smart about what you post. As discussed in Chapter 3, "What to Share—and What *Not* to Share—on Social Media," the more personal information you share, the more you put yourself at risk for identity theft, online harassing, and real-world burglary and assault. Do not post, however innocently or inadvertently, your street address, phone number, email address, Social Security number, or the like.

For that matter, don't post anything that bad guys could use to guess your password to this or other accounts. That means don't post your pet's name, your mother's maiden name, your favorite high school teacher, your favorite color, and the like. Don't make things easy for would-be hackers.

Don't Accept Every Friend Request

Social media encourage social interaction, so when you first sign up for a social network, you'll likely be bombarded by friend requests from people you barely remember. You don't have to say "yes" to all these requests; just because someone wants to be your friend doesn't mean you have to let them. Be choosy.

There's another reason not to blindly accept every friend request you receive. Some identity thieves like to create fake profiles in the hopes that people (like you!) will absent-mindedly accept them. Once in your friends list, these scammers have access to everything you post—which, if you aren't that smart about posting, can include private information the scammer can use to gain access to this or other online accounts.

And even if they're not crooks and thieves, don't assume that your online friends are your real friends. I have Facebook "friends" who I barely remember from high school. There are things I'd share with my real friends that I'd never in my life imagine sharing with these Facebook friends-in-name-only. Remember, a real friend is one you can email or call on the phone, not someone who may (or may not) read the stuff you post on Facebook.

It's Not All Good

Spoofed Accounts

Every so often I get a friend request from someone who's already on my friends list. What's up with that?

If you're not careful, you might go ahead and confirm the request without thinking twice about it. But that's the wrong thing to do because you're not confirming your real friend, the person you're already friends with, you're confirming some scamster who's *spoofed* your friend's account—profile picture and everything.

When you confirm a spoofed account, you open yourself up to all sorts of mischief. The spoofster might try to engage you in conversation and even try to hit you up for your personal information or perhaps a small loan. That's the way they work.

The proper response when you receive this sort of duplicate friend request is to *ignore* the request and report this phony friend to Facebook. You do this by clicking on the fake friend's name to go to the fake profile page. Click or tap on the More (three-dot) icon and select Give Feedback or Report This Profile. Follow the onscreen instructions to report the person as fake.

If you accidently confirmed the friend request, you should immediately go to the fake friend's page and unfriend that person. You can then report the fake friend to Facebook and let them do their thing.

Unfriend People Who Aren't Friendly

Just because you add someone to a social media friends list doesn't mean that person has to stay in your list. If you find someone is posting offensive messages, hijacking the comments on your messages, or just annoying you with too many cat pictures, you can "unfriend" that person. (*Unfriending* is the act of removing someone from a friends list.) In fact, it makes sense to cull your friends lists from time to time, to separate the wheat from the chaff. You want your news feeds to include interesting posts from people you care about, not be full of junk that doesn't matter to you.

Keep Your Contacts Private

Many social networking sites seek to help you add people to your friends list, by volunteering to sift through your email or phone contacts lists for people who are also on that social network. If you let a social network scan your address book or contacts list, the site might use this information to send advertisements (or advertisements disguised as "your friend likes" messages) to these friends. Not only are these fake endorsement messages annoying, they might be sent to people who are in your lists but who you don't actually communicate with on a daily basis.

It's best to keep your lists separate. Don't give social networks access to your phone or email contacts. It's not good policy.

Don't Download Third-Party Applications

Some social media, such as Facebook, enable third parties to install games and applications that extend the functionality of the sites. The problem is that many of these third-party apps gain access to and use your personal information (including the names in your friends list) in ways you might not approve of. Some rogue apps may even steal your personal information, including usernames and passwords.

If you want to minimize your risk, don't install third-party apps for your social networks. If you do find an app you like, read the reviews and ask around to make sure the app is legitimate—and not overly intrusive.

Don't Play Social Games

Along the same lines, some of the social games available on Facebook and other sites can be extremely intrusive in how they access and use your personal information and friends lists. You really don't want the latest game you played to post your score (or requests for extras or support) to all your friends' news feeds, do you? While social games can be fun to play, they also can be the most annoying things you do online.

The ultimate solution is to not install or play any social games, period. (Good luck with that.) Short of this Draconian measure, you should examine the private policies and settings for any social game you want to play, and configure the settings in the least obtrusive way possible—or, if you have no other choice, avoid the game completely. It isn't worth sacrificing your (and your friends') privacy for a little gaming fun.

Configure Your Privacy and Security Settings

Speaking of privacy, most social media allow you to configure your personal privacy and security settings. This enables you to determine who sees what you post and how the site uses your personal information. You need to learn about and configure the privacy and security settings for the social networks you use.

Facebook Privacy

Learn more about Facebook's privacy and security settings in Chapter 9, "Configuring Facebook's Privacy Settings."

Use Strong Passwords

When you create an account with a given social network, you create a username (sometimes your email address) and password. As with all online accounts, you want to make your password as secure as possible, to make it more difficult for bad guys to gain access to your account. Follow these tips to create more secure passwords:

- Longer passwords are more secure. An eight-character password is more secure than a six-character one.

- Combine capital and lowercase letters.

- Use a combination of letters, numbers, and special characters.

- Don't use easily guessable words, such as your last name, pet's name, your birthdate, and such.

- The best passwords appear to be totally random combinations of characters. (These are also the hardest passwords to remember, but still…)

I know, creating (and remembering!) a strong password is a pain in the lower extremities. So write them down so you don't forget, or use a password manager app—such as Blur (dnt.abine.com), Keeper (www.keepersecurity.com), or Sticky Password (www.stickypassword.com)—to remember your passwords for you.

Use Different Passwords for Each Account

If you have a Facebook account, Twitter account, and Pinterest account, create different passwords for each of them. If you use the same password for all accounts, anybody breaking into one of your accounts can gain access to all of them. (Similarly, don't use your Facebook account to log into other social media accounts; keep each account separate!)

Install Anti-Malware Tools on Your Device

Since viruses and spyware can be spread via social media, it's a good idea to install anti-malware tools on your computer or mobile device. And, while anti-malware protection is a good back stop, you also want to avoid clicking links in posts that may surreptitiously install malware on your system.

Trust Your Instincts

If you stumble across something suspicious in your news feed, trust your instincts and don't click that link or enter additional information. Don't get suckered into scams that request money or information or anything else. Social media are no more or less dangerous than the other social interactions you have in the outside world; there are bad guys out there, but you can avoid them by using your head. As I said earlier—don't be dumb!

Keeping Your Private Information Private

As you've learned, many of the potential hazards of social media revolve around personal information posted publicly. Since most social networks encourage you to enter some degree of private information about yourself (to facilitate more social interactions), it's possible that some or all of this information won't remain private.

Of first concern is the contact information you're required or just encouraged to enter, as well as any personal information you have in your profile for a given site. This can include your email address, street address, phone number, and so forth.

Fortunately, most social networks give you the option of hiding most of this information. Facebook, in particular, includes privacy settings that let you determine who can see what information—everyone (public), people on your friends list, or just yourself. You should use the site's privacy tools, discussed in Chapter 9, to hide as much personal information as possible from as many people as possible. And, of course, if such information is optional, you don't have to provide it in the first place.

Getting More Information About Online Privacy

If you'd like to learn more about protecting yourself online, check out *My Online Privacy for Seniors* by Jason Rich.

The other private information that may become public is anything you post as part of your regular status updates—what you did last night, who you're hanging out with, what you think of your family members or colleagues. These posts are typically public by default, which means that anyone can read them. As with your contact and profile information, however, you can employ the site's post-specific privacy settings to limit who can see the information in any given post. In this fashion, you can avoid full public disclosure of your private life if you so desire.

Again, be smart about how you configure your privacy settings and about what you post. The tools are yours to use—it's your responsibility to use them smartly.

>>>Go Further
HOW FACEBOOK USES YOUR PERSONAL INFORMATION

When we talk about social media security and privacy, it's good to look at Facebook, the Internet's largest social network. What Facebook does, others often mimic.

Unfortunately, the news isn't all good. That's because the personal information you provide to Facebook can be used by Facebook in a number of different ways—not all of which are to your benefit.

For example, Facebook can use your profile information—age, gender, education, and so forth—to display targeted third-party advertisements on your home page. Facebook also might track the other websites you visit and serve you ads based on the contents of those sites. These targeted ads might be marginally more appealing than generic advertisements, but are still, at least to some, a violation of privacy; Facebook uses your likes and dislikes for the company's benefit, to sell advertising.

Similarly, your profile information can be used for targeted invitations of various sorts. For example, Facebook might determine your interests from your profile data and invite you to play a particular game, use a certain application, join a given group, or add someone as a friend. These might be helpful invitations, but they still rely on the use of your private information.

It's also possible that Facebook will sell your personal information to interested third parties. (Facebook's privacy policy says it won't sell your information, but these things change—and not every social network is as restrictive as Facebook is.) Once Facebook (or another social network) sells the data to a particular company, you typically receive one or more email messages advertising that company's wares. This isn't spam, but it's still an annoying use or abuse of your private information.

Here's the rub: All of these uses of your private information are perfectly legal, and you probably agreed to them—assuming you read the fine print when you signed up for your account, of course. This points out the necessity of reading Facebook's terms of service before you sign up—and not participating if you don't like what you read.

Beyond these legal invasions of your privacy, there are many ways your personal information can be used illegally. These illegal invasions of your privacy can result in everything from spam to identity theft; you can guard against them by limiting the amount of personal information you publicly post on the social network site.

In this chapter, you discover the most popular social media in use today.

→ Examining Different Types of Social Media
→ Discovering the Top Social Media for Older Users

5

Comparing the Most Popular Social Media

I've talked a lot about Facebook, Pinterest, and Twitter, but there are a lot more social media than just these, and they all service slightly different purposes and user bases.

Examining Different Types of Social Media

Social media are those websites, services, and platforms that people use to share experiences and opinions with one another. They cover everything from social networks, where users share the details of their own lives, to social bookmarking services, where users share sites and articles they like.

Social Networks

The first type of social media is the *social network*. Social networks are unquestionably the most popular type of social media in use today.

A social network is a large website or service that hosts a community of users and facilitates public and private communication between those users. Social networks enable users to share experiences and opinions with each other via short posts or status updates.

Some social networks, such as school or alumni networks, are devoted to a specific topic or community. Other social networks, such as Facebook, are more broad-based, which allows for communities within the overall network to be devoted to specific topics.

Because of their multifaceted offerings, social networks appeal to a broad base of users. Young and old people alike use social networks, as do people of all genders, races, and income and education levels. Social networks help us keep up to date on what our friends are doing and keep our friends updated on what we are doing. Social networks also help establish a sense of community based on shared experiences at school, in the workplace, or at play.

Most social networks revolve around users' posts or status updates. Users keep their friends informed of current activities via these short text or picture posts and read updates posted by friends via some sort of news feed. Everybody keeps up to date with what everybody else is doing.

Many social networks also offer other means of user-to-user communication, including private email and one-to-one instant messaging. Most social networks also include various forms of media sharing, including digital photographs, videos, and the like.

The most popular social networks today are Facebook (www.facebook.com) and LinkedIn (www.linkedin.com).

Media Sharing Networks

A *media sharing network* like Pinterest or Instagram is a social network that focuses on images instead of text messages. There is less one-to-one communication and more general photo and video sharing. A media sharing network is like Facebook without all those bothersome words and sentences.

In a media sharing network, users post their own photos and videos or links to images on various web pages. Their friends and followers then view, comment on, and share those posts with other people. The most popular images go viral and are shared by thousands of interested users.

Because we've evolved into a very visual society, media sharing networks are becoming increasingly popular, particularly among users of mobile devices. It's easy to snap a picture with your smartphone and then post it to your network of choice. (For that matter, photo sharing on general social networks, such as Facebook and even Twitter, has become a very big part of the overall social experience.)

The most popular media sharing social networks today are Instagram (www. instagram.com), Pinterest (www.pinterest.com), and YouTube (www.youtube.com).

Microblogging Services

When you separate the short text messages or status updates from a social net-work into a separate feed, you have a *microblogging service*. Some microblogs, such as Twitter, exist primarily to distribute short text posts (and the occasional photo) from individual users to groups of followers; other microblogs, such as Tumblr, are more focused on posting images and longer text-based content.

Microblogs do not offer many of the community features found on larger social network sites. Most microblogs don't offer topic-based groups, photo stor-age and sharing, and the like. The primary service they offer is public message distribution.

With a typical microblogging service, registered users post short text messages, photos, or videos. Other users sign up to follow the posts of individual mem-bers and receive notifications when someone they follow makes a new post. Microblog posts are used to convey personal information and opinions; busi-nesses also use them to make commercial announcements.

Many of the most-followed microbloggers are celebrities; fans follow their posts to learn more about the celebrities' activities. Major news organizations also use microblogs to post breaking stories, whereas individuals post details of their per-sonal lives to interested friends and family followers.

The most popular microblogging services today are Twitter (www.twitter.com) and Tumblr (www.tumblr.com).

Message Boards and Comment Sections

Many websites offer *online message boards* or *comment sections* where users can interact by leaving their comments about general topics or specific articles. You can find message boards or comments sections on many general-interest and news-oriented sites, as well as on sites that focus on specific topics.

A message board is a public forum. Users can start a new topic or comment on an existing one. Comments are organized into *threads*, with each successive user adding his comments to those comments left by previous users. It's not real-time interaction, but it is a continuing discussion.

The advantage of frequenting a given site's message board as opposed to using a larger, more general social network is that you know you're interacting with people who like the same things you do. Message boards create a community of like-minded users, not unlike a traditional club or group, but not limited by physical boundaries. If you're a model kit builder, for example, a kit-building message board helps you keep in touch with kit builders from around the world.

Message Boards

Learn more about message boards in Chapter 17, "Getting Social on Special Interest Message Boards."

>>>Go Further
REDDIT

There's one social media site that doesn't fit cleanly in any of these buckets. Reddit (www.reddit.com) is a social website that lets users aggregate online content and facilitates discussion about that content. It's not really a social network; it's more like a collection of message boards organized around specific topic areas.

As such, the Reddit site is a hotbed of lively online conversation between users—such a hotbed that the site generates a lot of controversy. In fact, Reddit conversations are often so unruly—and sometimes vicious—that the site can be downright unfriendly to more genteel users. This is probably one reason why Reddit isn't widely used by older adults—although it's popular among many younger, more vocal users.

Discovering the Top Social Media

Of all the various social media available today, which should you be interested in? The answer, as you might suspect, is that it all depends.

You need to choose your social media based on what you're interested in and who you want to stay in touch with. For example, if you just want to stay in touch with your cousin Emily and her family, or the neighbors from your old neighborhood, or the folks you go to church with, then a general social network such as Facebook is the right choice. If, on the other hand, you want to keep in contact with your old business associates, then LinkedIn's professional networking makes more sense. If you like to share pictures of recipes and do-it-yourself (DIY) projects, consider Pinterest. Or if you want to stay hip with what your younger children or grandchildren are up to, then the youth-oriented Twitter is the place to be.

That said, some social media have more appeal to older users than do others. The following graphic details the percentage of online users aged 50 and up who use various social media.

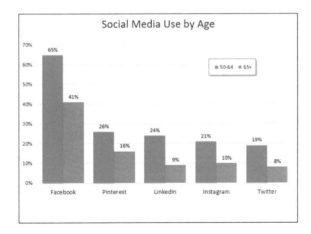

As you can see, Facebook is definitely the big dog among more mature users. If you use only one social medium, that's the one. But Pinterest and LinkedIn—and even Instagram and Twitter—also have appeal and might be worth considering. Let's take quick look at what each of these social media have to offer.

Facebook

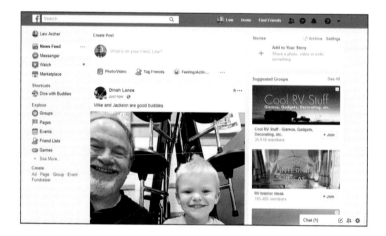

There are lots of reasons why Facebook (www.facebook.com) is used by the majority of online users over 50. It's big (more than 2.3 billion users each month), which means that most of your friends and family are already using it, so there are lots of people to interact with. It offers a variety of features that help you connect or reconnect with people you know or used to know. And it's easy to use and doesn't require a lot of technical or computer expertise. In short, it's the whole ball of wax in a very user-friendly package.

People use Facebook to keep their friends informed of their latest activities, as well as to keep in touch with what their friends are doing. The average adult Facebook user has more than 300 friends on the site and spends more than 35 minutes every day connected to the Facebook site.

Because of its general nature, Facebook is popular among people of all ages. Users range from grade schoolers (actually, the official minimum user age is 13) to retired snowbirds—with the older generation making up most of the site's growth in recent years.

In addition to posting and reading status updates, Facebook users have access to a variety of other community features. Facebook offers topic-oriented groups, pages for companies and celebrities, photo and video sharing, social games, instant text messages, one-to-one video chats, and even live video broadcasting. Many people log onto Facebook in the morning and stay logged in all day— there's that much to do there. And you can access all of Facebook's features from your computer, smartphone, or tablet.

In short, Facebook is the premier social medium for online users of all ages—and especially for those over age 50.

Facebook

Learn more about Facebook in Chapter 6, "Keeping in Touch with Friends and Family on Facebook."

Pinterest

Pinterest (www.pinterest.com) has risen to become the number-two social medium among older users, used by more than a quarter of those aged 50 to 64. In a way, Pinterest is like Facebook but with only pictures. Members use Pinterest to share photos and other images they find interesting with their family and online friends.

The way it works is you find an image from a website or another user, and then you "pin" that image to one of your personal boards on the Pinterest site. Other users see what you've pinned, and if they like it, they *repin* it to their boards.

A Pinterest board is like an old-fashioned corkboard, only online. Your boards become places where you can create and share collections of those things you like or find interesting. You can have as many boards as you want, organized by category or topic. It's a way to collect images you like and share them with the wider Pinterest community.

Pinterest is unique among today's social media in that it has been strongly embraced by women of all ages. More than 80% of Pinterest users are women, and half are over age 40. Pinterest users are more likely to live in Midwestern states instead of the coasts, and two-thirds are firmly middle-class.

The visual nature of Pinterest makes it attractive to non-technical users. It's the number-two social medium for older users, closely behind LinkedIn. If you're into collecting or recipes or DIY projects, Pinterest has a lot to offer.

Pinterest

Learn more about Pinterest in Chapter 12, "Pinning and Repinning on Pinterest."

LinkedIn

LinkedIn (www.linkedin.com) is a social network, like Facebook, but with a distinct focus on business. The site was launched in 2003 and currently has more than 500 million registered users. LinkedIn is the number-three social medium among users 50 to 64—and number-four among those 65 and older.

LinkedIn is used primarily by current and former business professionals for networking and job hunting. It's a great place to keep in touch with current and former co-workers, as well as others in your profession.

About a third of LinkedIn users are at least 50 years old. That's more than 150 million users aged 50 or older. Because of its professional focus, LinkedIn has a higher percentage of higher-income users than any other social media. Most

LinkedIn users are successful in their chosen professions, with close to half describing themselves as "decision-makers" in their companies.

In addition, millions of companies have LinkedIn Pages to establish a strong industry presence. LinkedIn also counts among its members executives from all Fortune 500 companies.

People use LinkedIn to expand their list of business contacts, keep in touch with colleagues, give and receive professional endorsements, and keep abreast of developments in their professions. Contacts made on LinkedIn can be used for a number of different purposes, such as finding employment, making a sale, or exploring business opportunities. You also can use LinkedIn to gain an introduction to a specific individual you'd like to know, via connections with mutual contacts.

In short, if you're a business professional, LinkedIn needs to be part of your social media portfolio. Compared to other social media, the overall tone and demeanor of this one is serious.

LinkedIn

Learn more about LinkedIn in Chapter 14, "Fine-Tuning Your Professional Profile on LinkedIn."

Twitter

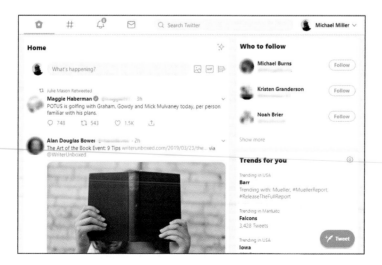

Twitter (www.twitter.com) is a microblogging service popular with people in their 20s and 30s and with those who like to follow celebrities and politicians. Users post relatively short (280-character) text messages, called *tweets*, from their computers or mobile phones; a tweet also can include a web link, picture, or video. Tweets are displayed to a user's followers and are searchable via the Twitter app or website.

Although Twitter gets a lot of media attention, it comes in as the fifth most-used social network for users of all ages, including those aged 50 to 64. Twitter currently has more than 300 million users each month who generate more than 500 million tweets each day. Only about a quarter of Twitter's users are older than age 50, however; perhaps because it's a bit more technically difficult to use, Twitter remains a social medium targeted at younger users.

Unlike Facebook, Twitter has few community-oriented features, which has also hindered the service's mainstream acceptance. Twitter is a microblogging service, not a full-featured social network. With Twitter, you only get message posting and following; there's no photo sharing or groups.

Given Twitter's limitations, why do younger people like it so much? Like Facebook, some people use Twitter to inform friends and family of what they're doing and thinking. Others use Twitter as a kind of personal blog, posting random thoughts and comments for all to read. Businesses use Twitter to promote their brands and products, making announcements via their Twitter feeds. Celebrities and entertainers (arguably the most-followed tweeters) use their Twitter feeds as a kind of public relations (PR) channel, feeding information of their comings and goings to their fan bases. As you've probably noticed, politicians (and presidents) also use Twitter to get their messages out to the faithful. And news organizations use Twitter to dissect the tweets of the rich and famous and disseminate the latest news headlines.

Most-Followed Celebrities

Reflecting the youth-oriented nature of Twitter, the top five most-followed Twitter accounts (as of March, 2019) are Katy Perry (@katyperry), Barack Obama (@BarackObama), Justin Bieber (@justinbieber), Rihanna (@rihanna), and Taylor Swift (@taylorswift13). Lady Gaga (@ladygaga) is number six, Ariana Grande (@ArianaGrande) is number eleven, and Donald Trump is number thirteen (@realDonaldTrump).

That last bit is important. Although Twitter is not a formal news medium, in that it has no central organization or paid reporters, it has become an important medium for disseminating breaking news stories. Today, many major news stories are tweeted before they're announced by the traditional news media, either by individuals on the scene or by reporters who can quickly tweet about an event before filing a lengthier news report.

So if you want to keep abreast of breaking news (both actual and celebrity-related), follow the pontification (or ravings) of your favorite politician, or just want to see what the younger generation is up to, give Twitter a spin. Otherwise, a more full-featured social network, such as Facebook, is probably a better choice.

Twitter

Learn more about Twitter in Chapter 10, "Following Interesting People on Twitter."

Instagram

Instagram (www.instagram.com) is the fourth most popular social medium among users aged 50 to 64. Unlike the other social media discussed here,

Instagram is primarily mobile-based; it's essentially a media sharing network based on a mobile app for Apple and Android phones and tablets. You use the Instagram app to take pictures and videos with the camera in your phone or tablet, and then you post those items to the Instagram network. The pictures and videos you post are viewed by your friends and followers and then shared with their friends and followers.

Although Instagram has a website, it's really mobile-based, as it relies on the pictures and videos you take with your smartphone. In fact, some people use the Instagram app solely for taking pictures, as it offers a variety of filters and special effects to enhance the photos you take.

People use Instagram to visually document their lives. When you do something of interest, you snap a picture and post it to Instagram. Your friends do the same. You don't need to read long, boring text posts—just look at pictures. There's an appeal to that—especially among younger users. To that end, 71% of Instagram's 1 billion or so users are aged 34 or younger; only 5% of all users are aged 55 and up.

Instagram's users are quite active, posting more than 100 million photos and videos each day. That makes Instagram one of the top photo-sharing services on the Internet—even without the social component.

Instagram

Learn more about Instagram in Chapter 16, "Sharing Photos with Instagram."

Michael Miller is at **Eastview High School**.

Yesterday at 6:16 PM · 🌐

Lael has her first soccer game of the season this evening. Perfect weather for it.

In this chapter, you learn how to use Facebook, the Internet's largest social network.

→ Signing Up and Signing In
→ Navigating Facebook
→ Finding Facebook Friends
→ Reading the News Feed
→ Posting Status Updates to Your Friends

6

Keeping in Touch with Friends and Family on Facebook

If you only join one social network, Facebook is the one. Facebook is the world's largest social network, a great place to keep in touch with family and friends wherever they live.

Signing Up and Signing In

When you're signed up as a Facebook member, you can post your own thoughts and comments, upload pictures to share, and even share your favorite web pages. Likewise, you can see what your friends and family are posting—their activities, photos, web links, and the like. That's why more than half of all online users aged 50 and up make Facebook their hub for online social activity—and check in at least an hour each day.

Facebook Mobile App

If you want to access Facebook from your smartphone or tablet, you need to download Facebook's mobile app for your device. Facebook has apps for Android and Apple's iOS (iPhone and iPad) devices. Download the app (for free) from your device's app store.

Create a New Facebook Account

To use Facebook, you first need to create a personal Facebook account. A Facebook account is free and easy to create; there's no fee to join and no monthly membership fees.

You can sign up from the Facebook website, using your notebook or desktop computer, or from the Facebook mobile app on your smartphone or tablet.

① To sign up from the Facebook website, go to www.facebook.com and enter your first and last names, email address or mobile phone number, desired password, birthdate, and gender. Click Create Account to proceed and follow the on-screen directions from there.

② To sign up from the Facebook mobile app, launch the app and tap Create New Facebook Account.

3. On the Join Facebook screen, tap Next. You are led through a series of screens that ask for specific information. You're prompted to allow access to your contacts and phone functions; enter your mobile phone number, birthday, and gender; create a password; add your email address to your account; save your password for single-tap login; add a profile picture; and look for possible friends in your phone's contacts. Follow the on-screen instructions to complete the sign-up.

Join Facebook

We'll help you create a new account in a few easy steps.

Next

3

Password Security

To make your password harder for hackers to guess, include a mix of alphabetic, numeric, and special characters, such as punctuation marks. You also can make your password more secure by making it longer; an eight-character password is much harder to crack than a six-character one. Just remember, though, that the more complex you make your password, the more difficult it may be for you to remember—which means you probably need to write it down somewhere, just in case. (And keep that written note hidden from prying eyes!)

Sign In to Facebook

The next time you go to the Facebook page on your computer or mobile device, you're prompted to sign in to your account. On subsequent visits, however, you stay logged in and don't have to enter anything.

1. To sign in from your computer, open your web browser and go to Facebook's home page at www.facebook.com. Enter your email address or phone number into the Email or Phone box, enter your password into the Password box, and then click the Log In button.

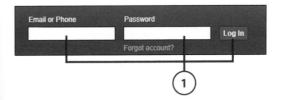

2. If you've signed in previously, you may see your account name and picture in a Recent Logins section. Click your name or picture, enter your password when prompted, and then click the Log In button.

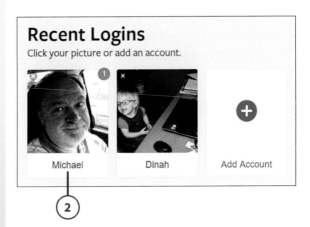

3. To sign in from your mobile phone or tablet, launch the Facebook app and tap your account. If you're prompted to enter your password, do so.

Sign Out of Your Facebook Account

You probably want to sign out of Facebook if you're not going to be active for an extended period of time. You also want to sign out if someone else in your household wants to access his or her Facebook account on your computer.

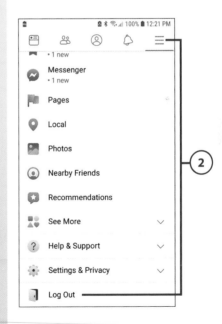

1. To sign out of Facebook from your computer, click the down arrow button at the far-right side of the toolbar, and then click Log Out from the drop-down menu.

2. To sign out of the Facebook mobile app, tap the More (three bar) icon, scroll to the bottom of the screen, and tap Log Out.

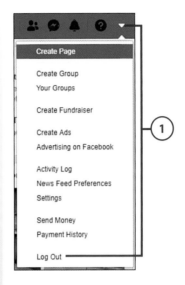

>>>Go Further

ABOUT FACEBOOK

Facebook is the brainchild of Mark Zuckerberg, an enterprising young man who came up with the concept while he was a student at Harvard in 2004. Facebook (called "thefacebook" at that time) was originally intended as a site where college students could socialize online. Sensing opportunity beyond the college market, Facebook opened its site to high school students in 2005 and then to all users over age 13 in 2006. Today, Facebook boasts more than 2.3 billion members worldwide.

Even though Facebook started out as a social network for college students, it isn't just for kids anymore. Today, just 20% of Facebook users are aged 24 or younger; 36% are aged 45 or older. In fact, Facebook's strongest growth in the past decade has come from users older than 55. (Take that, you young whippersnappers!)

Why are older adults using Facebook? Most (40%) use Facebook to connect with family and old friends; 30% use Facebook to share digital photos; and 20% play social games on Facebook. That makes Facebook both useful and fun—a great combination for users of any age.

Navigating Facebook

Facebook offers various features and functions that you access from different screens or pages on the website or app. Let's take a quick tour of what you'll find when you start exploring Facebook.

Navigate Facebook's Android App

Facebook offers mobile apps for each individual mobile platform. So there's a Facebook app for Android phones and tablets and different Facebook apps for iOS-based devices (iPhones and iPads). In most instances, the functionality is similar, even if the screen layout and navigation are slightly different.

This section describes Facebook's Android app. When you first open the app, you see the News Feed screen, which is as good a place as any to start.

1. Tap the News Feed icon to display the News Feed.

2. At the top of the news feed are "stories" from your friends. These are visual posts they've selected to share with their friends for a short period of time. Tap a story to view it.

3. Scroll down the screen to view posts from your friends. (Refresh the News Feed by pulling down from the top of the screen and then releasing.)

4. Tap What's on Your Mind? to post a status update.

5. Tap the Messenger icon to open the Messenger app and view or create one-on-one or group chats. (See the "Chatting with Facebook's Messenger App" sidebar, later in this chapter, for more information.)

6. Tap the Friends icon to view friend suggestions.

7 Tap the Profile icon to view your own profile page.

8 Tap the Notifications icon to view Facebook notifications, including friend requests.

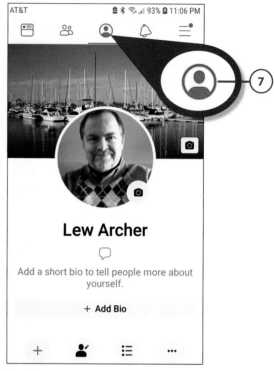

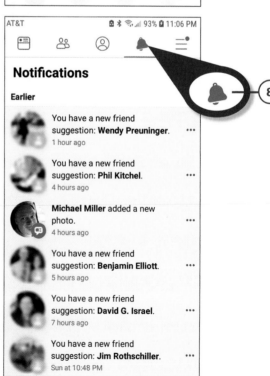

(9) Tap the More icon to view your favorite friends, pages, and groups, and to configure Facebook and app settings.

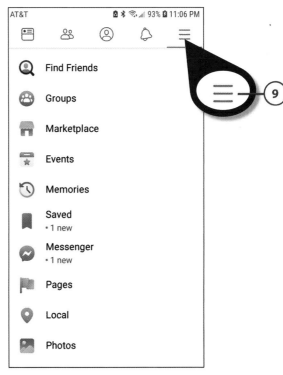

It Changes

Facebook and other social media tend to change the look and functionality of their apps a lot. I mean, *a lot*. It's likely that by the time you read this book, both the Android and iOS apps will have different icons along the top and bottom, and they'll maybe even present things in a different order. (For that matter, different users sometimes see different icons!) Be prepared for interface changes on a fairly regular basis. Facebook and other companies are constantly trying to improve their offerings, and you'll need to get used to that.

Navigate Facebook's iPhone App

Because of the different screen sizes on the iPhone and iPad, Facebook offers an app for each. The iPhone app looks a lot like the Android app, except with the navigation icons on the bottom instead of the top.

(1) Tap the News Feed icon at any time to display the News Feed screen.

(2) Tap the down arrow next to Stories to view "stories" (visual posts) from your friends.

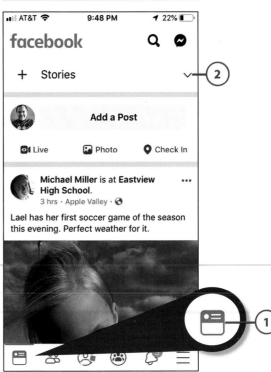

3 Scroll down the screen to view posts from your friends. (Refresh the News Feed by pulling down from the top of the screen and then releasing.)

4 Tap Add a Post to post a status update.

5 Tap the Messenger icon to open the Messenger app and chat with people in your friends list.

6 Tap the Friends icon to view friend suggestions.

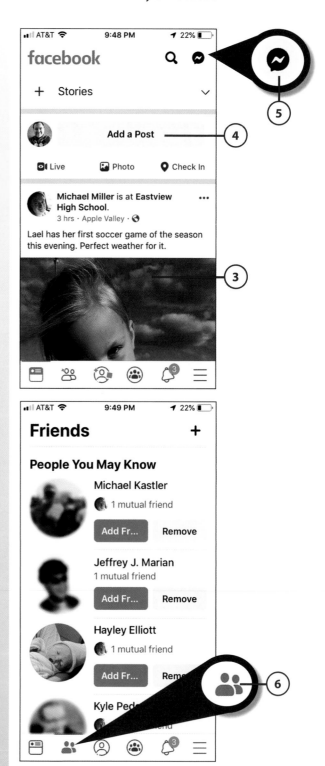

7 Tap the Profile icon to view your own profile page.

8 Tap the Groups icon to view your current and suggested groups.

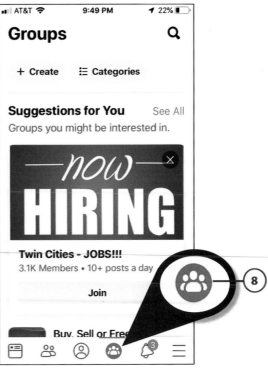

9 Tap the Notifications icon to view Facebook notifications.

10 Tap the More icon to view your favorite friends, pages, and groups, and to configure Facebook and app settings.

Mobile Website

You also can access Facebook using the web browser on your phone or tablet. Just open your device's web browser and enter the URL www.facebook.com; then you'll see the mobile version of Facebook's website. When you access the mobile site from your phone, it looks a lot like the mobile app; access it from your iPad and it looks more like the normal Facebook website.

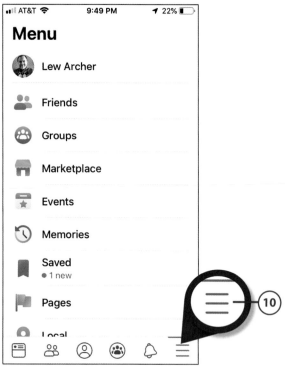

Navigate Facebook's iPad App

Facebook looks a little different on the bigger iPad screen than it does on the iPhone. It still does all the same things but with a slightly different layout.

When you first open the Facebook app on your iPad, you see the News Feed screen. How the screen looks depends on how you're holding your device.

1) In landscape mode (held horizontally), you see the News Feed on the left with a sidebar on the right side of the screen that displays a variety of different information, sometimes including upcoming events, the Chat panel (with favorite friends listed), trending topics, and more. Swipe up to scroll down the screen to view more updates in the News Feed.

2) In portrait mode (held vertically), you see the normal screen with no additional sidebars. All the navigation icons are at the bottom of the screen; tap News Feed to display the News Feed. Refresh the News Feed by pulling down the screen.

3) Tap What's on Your Mind? to post a status update.

4) Tap the down arrow in the top-right corner to access app settings.

5) Tap Messenger to open Facebook's Messenger app to chat with other Facebook users.

6 Tap Friends to view and respond to friend requests.

7 Tap Marketplace to view items for sale near you and to sell your own items.

8 Tap the Notifications icon to view notifications from Facebook.

9 Tap the More icon to view your favorite friends, pages, groups, and more.

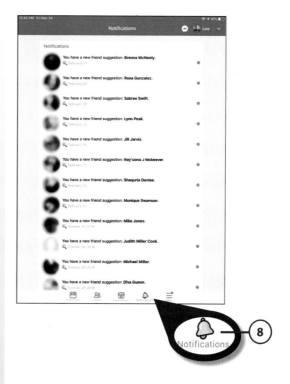

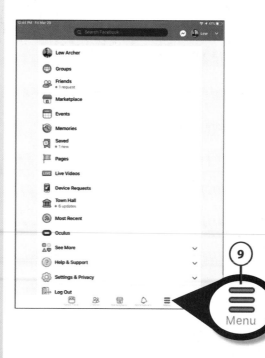

Navigate the Facebook Website on a Computer

To access Facebook on a desktop or notebook computer, you use your web browser. Go to www.facebook.com, sign in if necessary, and begin using Facebook.

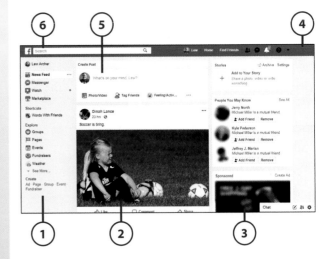

1 On the left side of the page is the *navigation sidebar*, or what Facebook calls the *left side menu*. You use the options here to go to various places on the Facebook site.

2 The large column in the middle of the home page displays your *News Feed*, a stream of posts from all your Facebook friends. (It also includes posts from companies, celebrities, and groups you've followed.)

3 The column on the right side of the page displays various Facebook notices and advertisements.

4 Along the top of the page is the *toolbar*. It contains various ways to navigate the Facebook site.

5 Click the text box (it typically says something like Write Something or What's on Your Mind?) to post a status update.

6 Search the Facebook site for people or things by entering your query into the Search box; click the search (magnifying glass) icon or press Enter on your computer keyboard to start the search.

7 Click your name or profile picture to view your personal profile page.

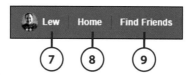

8 Click the Home button at any time to return to the Home page and your News Feed.

9 If your toolbar displays the Find Friends button (it probably will if you're new), click it to view suggested people for your Facebook friends list.

10 Click the Friend Requests button to view any friend requests you've received and to search for new friends on the Facebook site.

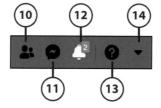

11 Click the Messages button to view your most recent private messages from Facebook friends.

12 Click the Notifications button to view notifications from Facebook, such as someone commenting on your status or accepting your friend request.

13 Click the Quick Help (question mark) icon to get help on using the Facebook site.

14 Click the down arrow button at the far right to access all sorts of account settings. This is also where you sign out of Facebook when you're done using it for the day.

Counting Requests and Messages

If you have pending friend requests, you see a white number in a red box on top of the Friend Requests button. (The number indicates how many requests you have.) Similarly, a white number in a red box on top of the Messages or Notifications buttons indicates how many unread messages or notifications you have.

Finding Facebook Friends

Facebook is all about connecting with people you know. Anyone you connect with on Facebook is called a *friend*. A Facebook friend can be a real friend, or a family member, colleague, acquaintance—you name it. When you add someone to your Facebook friends list, he sees everything you post—and you see everything he posts.

Find Friends on Your Phone

You can find new friends using the Facebook app on your phone or tablet, or you can go to the Facebook website. If you primarily use Facebook on your phone, that's the easiest way to search for people you know. This example uses Facebook's Android app.

1 Tap the More icon.

2 Tap Find Friends or Friends.

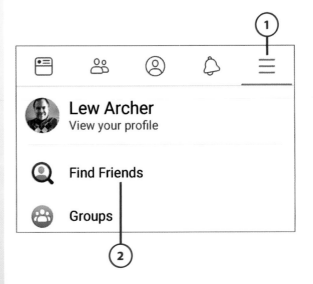

(3) Tap Suggestions to view people Facebook thinks might be friends—typically those who are friends with others you are friends with. (These folks are called *mutual friends*.)

(4) Tap Add Friend to send a friend request to any given person.

(5) Tap Search to search for someone by name.

(6) Begin to type a name into the Search box at the top of the screen. As you type, Facebook displays matching names. Tap to select a name.

(7) Tap the Add Friend icon next to the person you want.

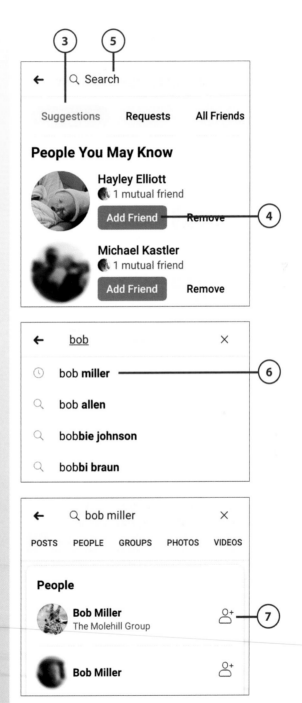

Find Friends on the Facebook Website

Although using the Facebook mobile app to find friends is convenient, you have a lot more options available when you do your searching on the Facebook website.

1 If you have a Find Friends button on the Facebook toolbar, click it. If not, click the Friend Requests button to display the drop-down menu, and then click Find Friends.

2 You see a page that lists any friend requests you've received and offers a number of friend suggestions from Facebook in the People You May Know section. Keep scrolling down the page to view more friend suggestions.

Suggested Friends

The people Facebook suggests as friends are typically people who went to the same schools you did, worked at the same companies you did, or are friends of your current friends.

3 To invite a person to your friends list, click the Add Friend button next to that person's name.

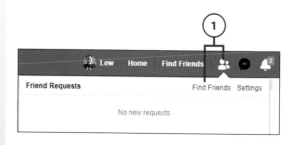

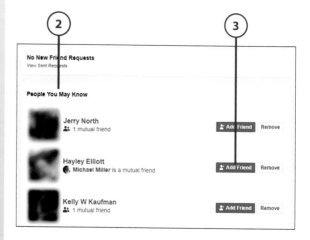

>>>Go Further
INVITATIONS

When you click the Add Friend button, Facebook doesn't automatically add that person to your friends list. Instead, that person receives an invitation to be your friend; she can accept or reject the invitation. If a person accepts your request, you become friends with that person. If a person does not accept your request, you don't become friends (nor are you notified if your friend request is declined). In other words, you both have to agree to be friends—it's not a one-sided thing.

Search for Friends

If Facebook doesn't automatically suggest a particular friend, there's still a good chance that person is already on Facebook and waiting for you to find her. It's your task to find that person—by searching the Facebook site.

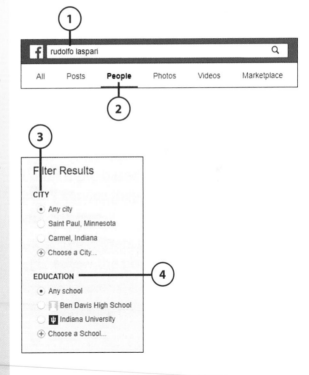

(1) Enter that person's name in the search box at the top of any Facebook page and then press Enter.

(2) On the search results page, click the People tab.

(3) You can filter the results by various criteria found in the left column. To search for people who live or came from a given city, go to the City section and select from the cities listed (typically your hometown and current city) or click Choose a City to enter a different locale.

(4) To search for people who went to the same high school or college you did, go to the Education section and check the name of the school or click Choose a School to enter a different school.

(5) To search for people who work
or worked for one of your current
or former employers, go to the
Work section and check the name
of that company or click Choose
a Company to select a different
employer.

(6) To search for people who are
already friends with your other
Facebook friends, go to the
Mutual Friends section and check
Friends. (You can also check
Friends of Friends to expand the
search to those who are friends
with the friends of your Facebook
friends.)

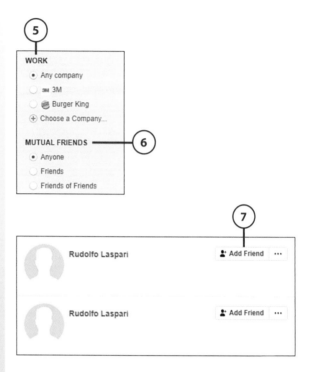

Multiple Filters

You can choose to filter your search on
more than one criteria. For example,
you can look for people who lived in
your hometown *and* work at a given
company, or who went to your college *and* live in your current city. Just
select multiple options in the Search for
Friends panel.

(7) Whichever options you select,
Facebook returns a list of suggested friends based on your
selection. Click the Add Friend
button to send a friend request to
a specific person.

Accept a Friend Request

Sometimes potential Facebook friends find you before you find them. When this happens, they send you a friend request, which you can then accept or decline. You can view friend requests within the Facebook app or on the Facebook website.

(1) On the Facebook website, click the Friend Requests button on the toolbar. All pending friend requests are displayed in the drop-down menu.

(2) Click Confirm to accept the request, or click Delete Request to decline the request.

(3) In the Facebook app, tap the Friends icon to open the Friends screen. All pending friend requests are displayed at the top of this screen.

(4) Tap Confirm to accept the request, or Delete to decline the request.

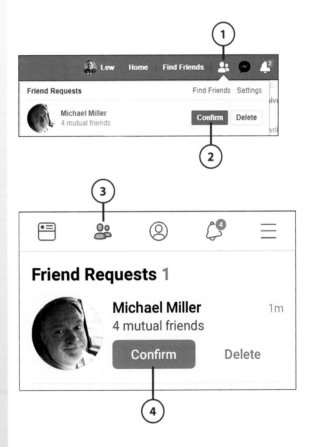

No One Knows

When you decline a friend request, the sender is not notified by Facebook. That person doesn't know that you've declined the request; he knows only that you haven't (yet) accepted it. The same thing when you unfriend a friend; he or she is not notified when you sever the connection.

Unfriend a Friend

You can, at any time, remove any individual from your Facebook friends list. This is called *unfriending* the person, and it happens all the time.

1. From the Facebook app, tap the Profile icon to open your profile page, and then scroll to the Friends section.

2. If necessary, tap See All Friends, and then scroll to the person you want to unfriend and tap that person's name or thumbnail photo.

3. Tap Friends.

4. Tap Unfriend.

Unfollow

If you want to stay friends with a person but don't want to see all their posts in your News Feed, select to Unfollow instead of Unfriend. You'll stay friends but won't be bothered by their posts.

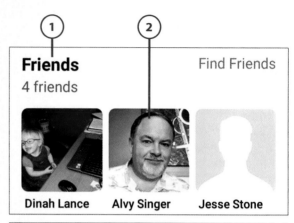

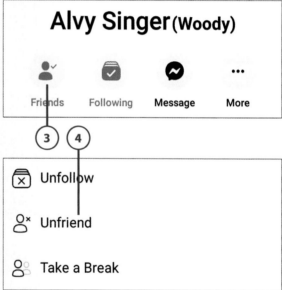

Reading the News Feed

Facebook's News Feed is where you keep abreast of what all your friends are up to. The News Feed consists of status updates made by your friends and by companies and celebrities you've liked on Facebook. It also includes posts from Facebook groups you've joined, as well as the occasional advertisement.

View Status Updates

Status updates are displayed in your News Feed in rough reverse chrono-logical order, newest first. I say "rough" order because Facebook attempts to determine which posts are of most interest to you and gives them more prominent placement. Also, posts with recent comments also are displayed more prominently in the feed.

(1) Tap or click Home to display the News Feed.

(2) Scroll down the page or screen to view additional posts.

(3) The profile picture of the person who is posting (called the poster) appears in the top-left corner of the status update.

(4) The poster's name appears at the top of the post, beside the profile picture. To view the poster's pro-file page, click or tap the person's name.

(5) When the item was posted is displayed beneath the poster's name.

(6) The content of the status update appears under this top portion of the post. This can include text, images, or a video.

(7) Links to like, comment on, and share this post appear after the post content.

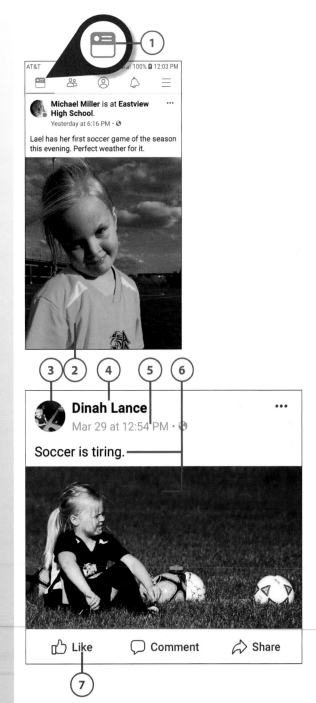

View Links to Web Pages

Many status updates include links to interesting web pages. You can click a link to view the web page posted by your friend.

(1) The title of the linked-to web page appears under the normal status update text. Click the URL in the text or the page title to display the linked-to web page.

(2) Many links include images from the linked-to page, as well as a short description of the page's content.

Like and Comment on an Update

Facebook is a social network, which means you can interact socially with the status updates your friends make. You can tell your friend you "like" a given post, you can comment on a post, and you can even share a post with other friends.

When you "like" a friend's status update, you give it a virtual "thumbs up." It's like voting on a post; when you view a status update, you see the number of "likes" that post has received.

(1) Like an update by clicking or tapping Like. (The number of other people who have liked this status update is displayed next to the Like icon; click this to see who has liked the post.)

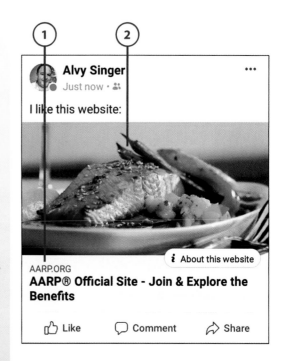

2 Comment on an update by clicking or tapping Comment and then typing your comment.

Share an Update

Occasionally, you find a status update that is interesting or intriguing enough you want to share it with all of your friends. You do this via Facebook's Share feature.

1 Click or tap Share underneath the original post.

2 Enter any comments you have about this post and then click or tap the Share Now or Post button.

Posting Status Updates to Your Friends

To let your family and friends know what you've been up to, you need to post what Facebook calls a *status update*. Every status update you make is broadcast to everyone on your friends list by being displayed in their News Feeds on their home pages. It's how they know what you've been doing and thinking about.

Post a Status Update

A status update is, at its most basic, a brief text message. It can be as short as a word or two, or it can be several paragraphs long; that's up to you. (Facebook lets you post updates with more than 60,000 characters, which should be more than long enough for most of us.)

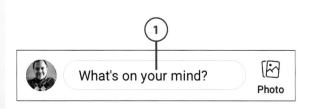

1. From the top of the Facebook home page or screen, click or tap What's on Your Mind?

2. A new panel or screen for creating your post opens. Type your message here.

3. Tap or click Photo/Video to add photos or a video stored on your device to your post.

4. Tap or click Tag Friends to mention or "tag" friends in the post. (The resulting post includes a link to the tagged person or persons.)

5. Tap or click Feeling/Activity/Sticker to add an emoji to your post indicating how you're currently feeling or what you're currently doing.

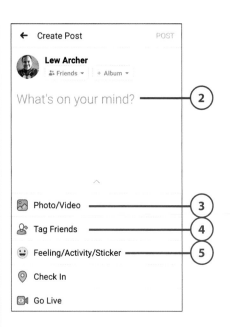

6 Tap or click Check In to add your current location to the post.

7 Tap Go Live (in the mobile app) or click Live Video (on the website) to start broadcasting a live video from your phone or computer webcam.

8 Tap or click Post or Share to post the update when you're ready.

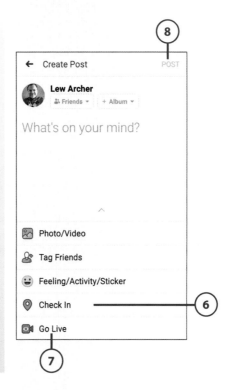

It's Not All Good

Don't Publicize Your Location

You might not want to identify your location on every post you make. If you post while you're away from home, you're letting potential burglars know that your house is empty. You're also telling potential stalkers where they can find you. For these reasons, use caution when posting your location in your status updates.

Post a Link to a Web Page

You can include links to other web pages in your status updates. Not only does Facebook add a link to the specified page, it also lets you include a thumbnail image from that page with the status update.

1. Start a new post as normal, and enter any accompanying text.

2. Enter the URL (web address) for the page you want to link to as part of your update.

3. Facebook should recognize the link and display a thumbnail image from the page. (In some instances, you may be able to choose from two or more images from the page.)

4. Click Post or Share when done.

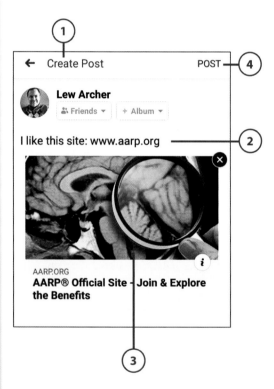

>>>*Go Further*

CHATTING WITH FACEBOOK'S MESSENGER APP

Facebook lets you send messages directly to individual friends or groups of friends—but not within the Facebook mobile app. To message or chat with your friends from your phone or tablet, you need to install Facebook's Messenger app. (Like the main Facebook app, you can download Messenger for free from your device's app store.)

Once you've installed the Messenger app, chatting is as easy as selecting one or more people to talk with, and then typing away. You can even turn normal text-based chats into audio or video calls that take place over the Internet. Naturally, you can only chat with friends who are online the same time as you.

If you're using a computer, you can still chat with others from the Facebook website. Just click the Messages icon on the toolbar to select one or more people to chat with; your chats appear in a separate chat panel on the Facebook page.

In this chapter, you discover how to share digital photographs and videos via Facebook.

→ Viewing Friends' Photos and Videos
→ Sharing Your Own Photos and Videos

Sharing Pictures and Videos on Facebook

Before everybody got on the Internet, if you wanted to share photos with your family or friends, you had to make prints and mail them out to everyone, or invite everybody over to your house for an old-fashioned slide show. Today, however, you can share your photos online—and one way is via Facebook.

And Facebook is also a great place to share any home movies you've taken with your smartphone or camcorder. It's easy to upload photos and videos to Facebook and then share them with all your Facebook friends. Not surprisingly, it's equally easy to view your friends' photos and videos on Facebook.

Viewing Friends' Photos and Videos

Some people on Facebook post photos and videos as part of their regular status updates. These photos appear in your News Feed as part of the stream of your friends' status updates.

Other Facebook users post photos to special photo albums they've created in their Facebook accounts. This is a more serious and organized way to share a large number of photos online. You can view these photo albums from the user's Timeline page.

View Photos in Your News Feed

When a friend posts a photo as part of a status update, that photo appears in your News Feed. You can view photos at that small size within the News Feed or enlarge them to view them full screen.

(1) Within your News Feed, all photos appear within the bodies of the accompanying status updates. (A post can have multiple photos attached.) To view a larger version of any picture, click or tap the photo in the post.

(2) If you're using the Facebook website, this displays the photo within its own *lightbox*—a special window superimposed over the News Feed. To view the photo even larger, click the Enter Fullscreen icon at the top-right corner of the photo. (To exit fullscreen mode, press Esc on your computer keyboard or the X at the top-right corner of the screen.)

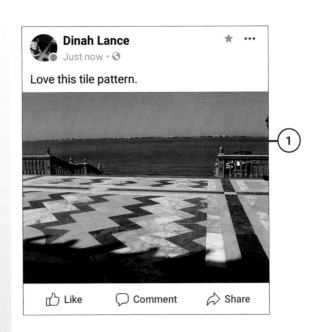

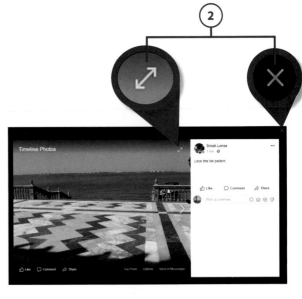

3 If you're using the Facebook mobile app, you see the photo on its own photo page. Press the Back button on your device to return to the News Feed. (Or, in the iOS app, tap the X in the upper-left corner.)

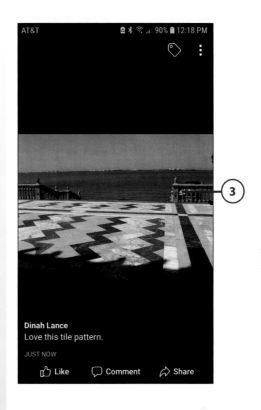

View Videos in Your News Feed

Viewing videos on Facebook is similar to viewing photos. When one of your friends uploads a video to Facebook, it shows up in your News Feed as a thumbnail image with a playback arrow in the middle of it. Playing a video is as easy as clicking that image.

1 Navigate to the status update that contains the video and then click the video thumbnail to play the video. In some cases, video playback begins in the News Feed itself. In other cases, playback begins in a separate video player similar to Facebook's photo light-box. (The video may play auto-matically when you scroll to the post, but without sound—kind of like a muted preview. If this is the case, you need to click or tap the video to play it back with sound.)

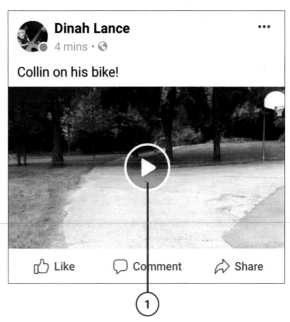

(2) If you want to view the video at a larger size on the Facebook website, mouse over the video to display the playback controls at the bottom, and then click the Full Screen icon. Click Esc on your computer keyboard to return to normal playback mode.

(3) To pause the playback on the Facebook website, mouse over the video to display the playback controls and then click the Pause button; the button changes to a Play button. To pause the play-back in the Android mobile app, just tap the screen. (In the iOS app, you have to tap the Pause button.) Click or tap the Play button or tap the screen again to resume playback.

(4) Click and drag (or tap and drag) the time slider to move to anoth-er point in the video.

YouTube Videos

If someone has posted a video from YouTube, Vimeo, or another video-sharing site, playback will probably take place within the News Feed. To view the video on the YouTube or Vimeo site, click or tap the title of the video to open that site in a new tab in your web browser or in the appropriate app on your mobile device. (Click or tap the video itself, and it plays within the News Feed.)

View a Friend's Photo Albums

More serious photographers—and those people with lots of photos to share—organize their Facebook photos into separate photo albums. These are virtual versions of those traditional photo albums you've kept in the past. You can navigate through a friend's photo albums to find and view the photos you like.

All the videos a friend uploads are stored in a special photo album labeled Videos. You can play back any video from there.

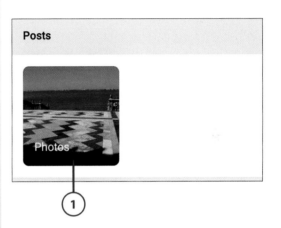

(1) Click or tap your friend's name or profile picture anywhere on Facebook to open her profile page. On the Facebook website, click Photos. In the Facebook app, scroll to the Posts section and tap the Photos tile.

(2) Click or tap Photos or Photos of *Friend* to view individual photos of your friend.

(**3**) Click or tap Albums to view photos as posted in their photo albums.

(**4**) Click or tap to open the selected album. (Videos are located in the Videos album.)

Share a Photo or Video

If you really like a friend's photo or video, you can share that item with your Facebook friends.

Privacy Settings

You can't share everything you see on Facebook. Some people configure their privacy settings so that photos and videos can be shared only with friends, or not shared at all.

(**1**) Display the photo or video and click or tap Share.

(**2**) Enter a description of the photo into the Say Something About This or Write Something box.

(**3**) Click the Privacy button and select who can view this photo.

(**4**) Click Post (or Share Now in the iOS app) to post this item to your timeline.

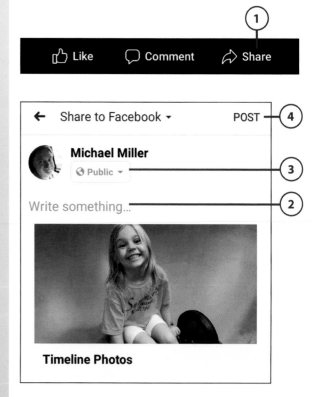

Download a Photo

If you find a friend's photo that you really like, you can download it to your computer or mobile device for your own use. (Be careful not to download or use for commercial use any photos that are copyrighted.)

1. On the Facebook website, click to open the photo and mouse over the photo to display the menu at the bottom of the photo. Click Options, and then click Download. If you're prompted to open or save the file, click Save.

2. In the Android mobile app, tap to display the photo. Then press and hold the photo and tap Save to Phone. In the iOS app, tap the photo, and then tap the Menu (three dots) icon and tap Save Photo.

Sharing Your Own Photos and Videos

We're taking more pictures than ever before, and we're doing it with our smartphones, tablets, and digital cameras. It's easy to take out your device and snap a few digital pictures, or even take a short video. Everybody's doing it.

It's equally easy to share all those pictures and videos with your friends on Facebook. You can do it directly from your phone, or from your computer.

Share a Photo or Video from Your Mobile Phone

The easiest way to share those photos you take with your phone is from your phone, using the Facebook mobile app. (This example uses Facebook's Android app; the iOS app works similarly.)

(1) Use your phone's camera to take a picture or video and then tap to open that picture in your phone's photo or gallery app.

(2) Tap Share. (This may look different on different phones.)

(3) Tap Facebook.

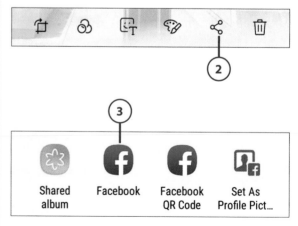

Shared album   Facebook   Facebook QR Code   Set As Profile Pict...

4 Say something about this photo, if you want.

5 Tap Share (or Next in the iOS app) to post the photo as a status update.

6 When prompted, check to share to your News Feed, to Your Story, or to both. (You probably want to share to your News Feed.)

7 Tap Share Now (Android) or Share (iOS).

Uploading from the Gallery

You also can upload photos you've taken previously from your phone's picture gallery. Just navigate to and open the photo you want to post; then tap Share and proceed from there.

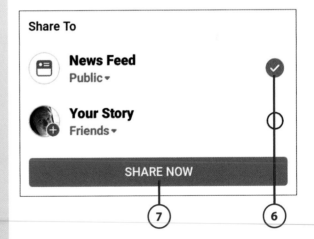

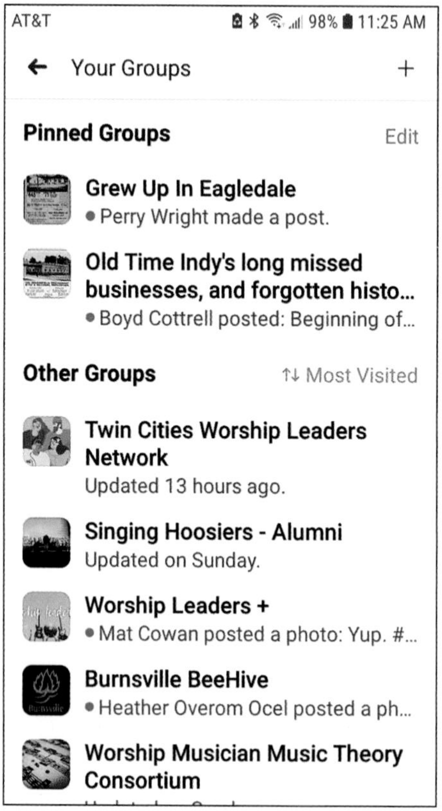

←   **Your Groups**   +

Pinned Groups   Edit

Grew Up In Eagledale
● Perry Wright made a post.

**Old Time Indy's long missed
businesses, and forgotten histo...**
● Boyd Cottrell posted: Beginning of...

Other Groups   ↑↓ Most Visited

**Twin Cities Worship Leaders
Network**
Updated 13 hours ago.

Singing Hoosiers - Alumni
Updated on Sunday.

Worship Leaders +
● Mat Cowan posted a photo: Yup. #...

Burnsville BeeHive
● Heather Overom Ocel posted a ph...

**Worship Musician Music Theory
Consortium**

8

Discovering Interesting Groups on Facebook

If you want to make new friends—and reconnect with old ones—one of the best ways to do so is to search out others who share your interests. If you're into gardening, look for gardeners. If you're into recreational vehicles, look for fellow RVers. If you're a wine lover, look for other connoisseurs of the grape.

You also can look for people who've shared your life experiences. That means connecting with people who went to the same schools, lived in the same neighborhoods, and participated in the same activities.

You can find people who share your history and hobbies in Facebook groups. A group takes the form of a special Facebook page, a place for people interested in that topic to meet online and exchange information and pleasantries.

Participating in Facebook Groups

A Facebook group is a special page devoted to a particular topic. You can find groups for various sports, hobbies, and activities, as well as those devoted to particular times and places, such as your old neighborhood when you were a kid.

Search for Groups

Facebook offers tens of thousands of different groups online, so chances are you can find one or more that suit you. The key is finding a particular group that matches what you're interested in—which you do by searching.

1. Go to the Facebook search box (on either the website or in the mobile app) and enter one or more keywords that describe what you're looking for. For example, if you're interested in golfing, enter **golf**. If you're looking for a group for graduates from your old high school, enter **high school name alumni**. (Replace *high school name* with the name of your high school, of course.) If you want to find a group created by people who live on the west side of Indianapolis, enter **Indianapolis west side**.

2. Scroll to the Categories section to browse groups by category.

3. Click a category tile to view groups in that category.

4. On the next screen, select the Groups tab.

5. Tap or click a group name to learn more about that group. *Or…*

6. Tap or click the + sign to join a group.

Browse For and Join Groups

There are several ways to browse for Facebook groups—by following Facebook's suggestions, exploring groups that your friends belong to, and viewing groups for your local area. You can do this from the Facebook app or the website, although it's a little easier from the website.

1. On Facebook's website, click Groups in the Explore section of the left-side navigation sidebar.

In the Mobile App
To discover groups in the Facebook mobile app, tap the More (three dot) menu, tap Groups, and then tap Discover.

2. Scroll to the Categories section to browse groups by category.

3. Click a category tile to view groups in that category.

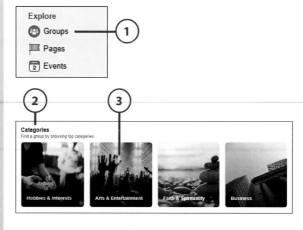

④ Scroll to the Friends Groups section to view groups that your Facebook friends have joined. Click any group name to visit that group's page, or click Join to immediately join a given group.

⑤ Scroll to the Popular Near You Groups section to view groups located in your area, such as those for local schools, organizations, and towns.

④

Friends' Groups
Groups your friends are in.

Apple Valley/Lakeville Area Swap and Shop
21K Members • 10+ posts a day   Join

Narrative Lectionary
6.9K Members • 10 posts a day   Join

Birthing Cross+Gen Community
5.9K Members • 3 posts a day   Join

Minnesota Music Scene
5.3K Members • 10+ posts a day   Join

⑤

Popular Near You
Groups people in your area are in

MN mushroom/morel Hunters & foragers
9.5K Members • 10+ posts a day   Join

Minneapolis/St. Paul Aviation Spotting
5.4K Members • 10+ posts a day   Join

Minnesota Through the Lens
4.3K Members • 10+ posts a day   Join

Old South Minneapolis
17K Members • 10+ posts a day   Join

>>>Go Further
PUBLIC AND CLOSED GROUPS

Most groups are classified as Public groups, meaning they're open for all Facebook members to join. Some groups, however, are Closed groups, which require that the group administrator approve all requests for membership.

To join a Closed group, you must apply for membership and hope that your request is granted. When you click or tap the Join button, a request goes to the group administrator. If your request is granted, you receive a message that you've been approved and are now an official member of the group. If your request is not granted, you don't get any response.

Visit a Group Page

Although you can view a feed of messages from all your groups (covered later in this chapter), most people prefer to visit individual group pages. This enables you to partake in all of the resources available in a given group.

1. On the Facebook website, click Groups in the Explore section of the left-side navigation sidebar.

2. In the Facebook mobile app, tap the More button.

3. Scroll down and tap Groups.

4. Click or tap the Groups tab to view all the groups to which you subscribe.

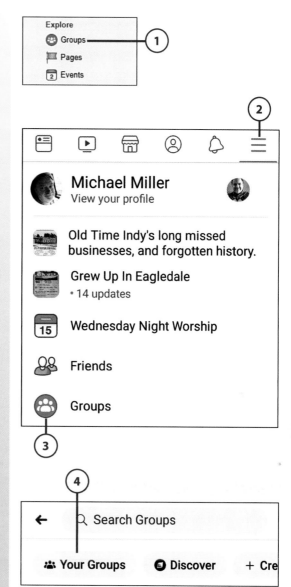

5 Click or tap the name of a group to open its Facebook page.

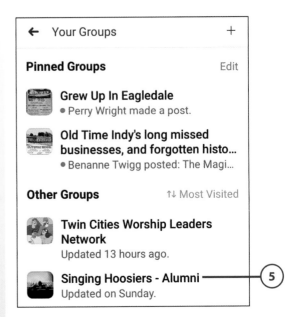

Read and Reply to Group Posts

After you open a group page, you can read posts from other members of the group and then like and comment on those posts as you would normal Facebook status updates.

Group Posts

Posts that you make on a group's Facebook page might be displayed only on that page, not in individual members' News Feeds, depending on their Facebook settings.

1 Open the group's page and view all posts from members in the scrolling feed.

2 Click or tap Like to like a particular post.

3 Click or tap Comment to reply to a post and then enter your reply into the Comment box.

Post to the Group

Not only can you reply to posts made by other members, you can start a new discussion by posting a new message on the group's page. Other group members can then like and reply to your message.

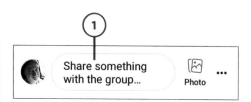

Moderated Groups

In some groups, the posts are moderated, so they must be approved by the group's moderator before they're seen by others.

(1) Open the group's page, scroll to the Publisher box, and click or tap Share Something with the Group. (In the iOS app, skip this step.)

(2) Enter your message into the What's on Your Mind? or Write Something box.

(3) Click or tap Photo/Video to add one or more photographs (or a single video) to this post.

(4) Click or tap Post to post your message to the group.

View Group Members

Who belongs to this particular group? It's easy to view all the members of a Facebook group.

(1) On the Facebook website, open the group's page and, in the left-hand column, click Members to display a list of group members.

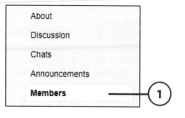

(2) In the Facebook app, open the group's page and tap the thumbnails of the group members.

(3) Tap or click any member's name to view that person's profile page. (In the iOS app, tap the name and then select View Profile.)

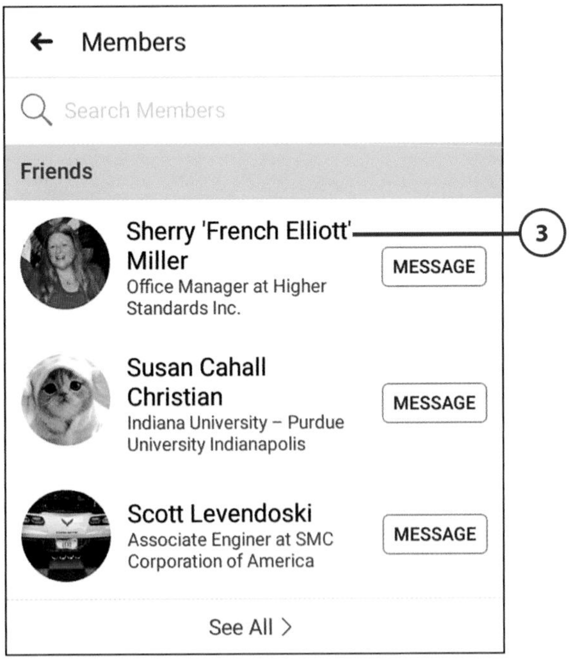

Ben Davis High School Class of 1975 >

PUBLIC GROUP · 288 MEMBERS

+ Invite

← Members

Q Search Members

Friends

Sherry 'French Elliott' Miller
Office Manager at Higher Standards Inc.

MESSAGE

Susan Cahall Christian
Indiana University – Purdue University Indianapolis

MESSAGE

Scott Levendoski
Associate Enginer at SMC Corporation of America

MESSAGE

See All >

Get Notified of Group Activity

If you're active in a Facebook group, you might want to be notified when others post to the group. You can opt to receive notifications of each post made, or only of those posts made by your friends.

(1) In the Facebook mobile app, open the group's page and tap More (three dots) in the top-right corner.

(2) Tap Notifications.

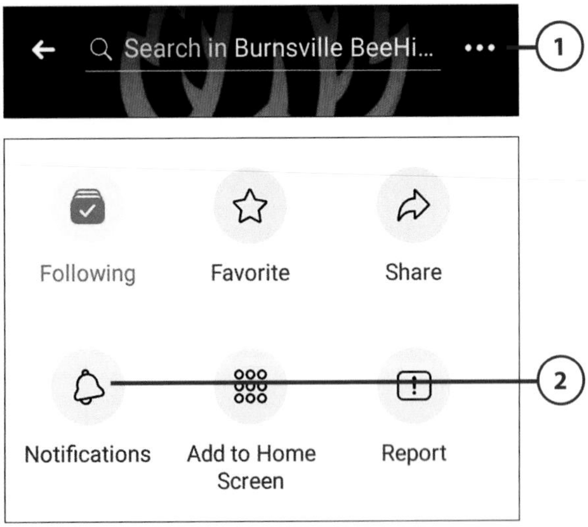

← Q Search in Burnsville BeeHi... •••

Following   Favorite   Share

Notifications   Add to Home Screen   Report

3 To receive a notification whenever a post is made to the group, go to the In-App section and select All Posts. To receive notification of the most important posts, select Highlights. To receive a notification whenever one of your Facebook friends posts to this group, select Friends' Posts. To receive no notifications from this group, select Off.

4 If you opt to receive any type of notification, you can then opt to receive push notifications (alerts on your phone) if you like. Go to the Push Notifications section and select Highlights or Off.

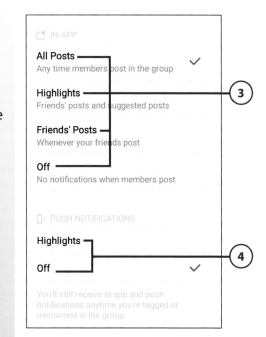

Leave a Group

If you grow tired of irrelevant or uninteresting posts in a given group, you can choose to unsubscribe from or leave a group.

1 In the Facebook mobile app, open the group's page and tap More (three dots in the top-right corner).

2 Tap Following to no longer see posts from this group.

3 Tap Leave Group to completely leave the group.

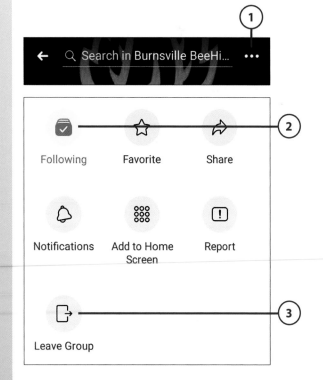

(4) On the Facebook website, open the group's page and click Joined.

(5) Click Unfollow Group to no longer see posts from this group.

(6) Click Leave Group to completely leave the group.

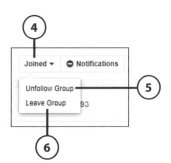

>>>Go Further

USING GROUPS TO RECONNECT WITH OLD FRIENDS

On the surface, it's easy to think of Facebook groups as twenty-first-century versions of the clubs you had back in high school. You know, chess club, knitting club, model airplane club, and the like.

Although there certainly are a huge number of these club-like Facebook groups, there are also groups that are more about times and places than they are about hobbies and interests. As such, these groups attempt to reconnect people with shared experiences.

I belong to a number of groups that connect me to the days of my youth. For example, I grew up on the west side of Indianapolis, and there's a Facebook group called Growing Up on Indy's Westside to which I belong. It's a fun little group, with people posting faded pictures of old haunts and lots of discussions about the way things used to be and what we used to do back then. I can't say I contribute too often, but it's always fun to read what others post.

I also belong to a "Where is and/or who do you remember?" group for my high school. This is a great place to find out what my old classmates have been up to in the decades since graduation. There are lots of posts asking about individual students, teachers, and events. It's a nice stroll down memory lane.

The point is, participating in Facebook groups can be a great way to reconnect with your past. You might even meet up with some of your old friends in these groups, or make some new friends you should have made way back then. It's kind of a virtual blast from the past, and we have the Facebook social network to thank for it.

Following Companies and Celebrities on Facebook

Even though businesses, celebrities, and public figures aren't regular users, they still want to use Facebook to connect with their customers and fans. They do this through Facebook Pages. If you're a customer or fan of a given company or celebrity, you can "like" that entity's Facebook page—and keep abreast of what that company or individual is up to. It's kind of like joining an online fan club through Facebook.

Search for Companies and Public Figures

Many companies and organizations have Facebook Pages for their brands and the products they sell. For example, you can find and follow Pages for AARP, McDonald's, Starbucks, UNICEF, Walmart, and similar entities.

Many famous people—entertainers, athletes, news reporters, politicians, and the like—also have Facebook Pages. So if you're a fan of James Taylor, Tom Hanks, Martha Stewart, or Sean Hannity, you can follow any or all of them via their Facebook Pages.

1. Enter one or more keywords that describe the person, company, or organization into the Search box.

2. Scroll to the bottom of the search results and tap or click See Results or See All Results.

3. Scroll through the tabs at the top of the screen and click or tap Pages.

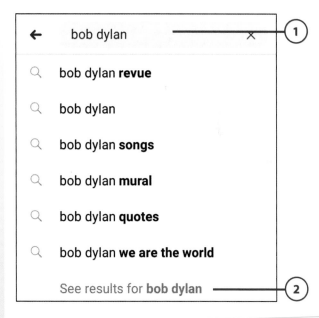

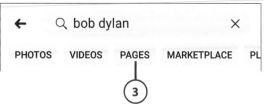

(4) Click or tap the name of the Page you want to view. *Or…*

(5) Click or tap Like (thumbs-up) to view posts from this page in your News Feed.

Local Pages

Facebook Pages aren't reserved for big public companies and celebrities. Many cities, libraries, schools, and even neighborhood associations have their own Facebook Pages. You often can find local events and discounts by visiting these local Pages. Many local stores and restaurants have their own Facebook Pages, too.

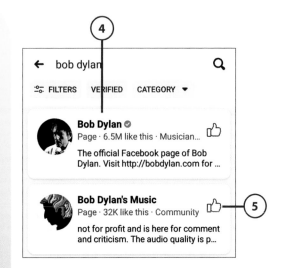

View a Facebook Page

A professional Facebook Page is very similar to a personal profile page, right down to the timeline of updates and activities. Pages can feature specialized content, however, which is located at the top of the page, under the cover image. For example, a musician's page might feature an audio player for that performer's songs; other pages might let you view pictures and videos, or even purchase items online.

(1) Click or tap About to read more about this person or organization.

(2) Click or tap Posts to read posts on this Page.

(3) Click or tap Photos to view the Page's official pictures.

(4) Click or tap Videos to view any videos from this person or organization.

>>>*Go Further*

PROMOTED VERSUS ORGANIC POSTS

Facebook used to display all posts from those Pages you like in your News Feed. It doesn't do that anymore. That's because Facebook is in the business of making money, and one way it does that is to charge companies to "promote" their Page posts.

When a post is promoted (that is, paid for), Facebook will display it in the News Feeds of all that page's followers. If a post is not promoted, Facebook probably won't display that post. If a company wants its followers to see its posts, it pretty much has to pay for that privilege.

Although some nonpromoted posts may show up in your News Feed from time to time, Facebook displays less than 20% of a Page's "organic" (nonpaid) posts. In other words, "liking" a given Page does not guarantee that you'll see all (or even most) of the posts to that Page. If you want to see all that a company or person is posting, you have to go to that Page to read the posts directly.

←   Privacy Shortcuts

Tools to help you control your privacy
and security on Facebook

Privacy

Control who sees what you
share on Facebook, and manage
data that helps us personalize
experiences.

🔒   Review a few important privacy
      settings

🎓   Learn about your privacy on
      Facebook

Configuring Facebook's Privacy Settings

Social media are social media, which means they're all about sharing one's personal information with others. If you'd rather not share everything with everybody—if you want to keep some private things private—then you need to configure the privacy settings for each social media network you use.

You learned the basics of social media privacy in Chapter 4, "Using Social Media—Safely and Privately." Because Facebook is the world's largest social network, and the one most used by those over age 50, it's worth exploring Facebook's various privacy settings. Configuring these settings is essential if you don't want all your personal information made public.

What Facebook Tracks—and Why

All the information that you share and that Facebook collects poses a problem if you'd rather keep some things private. If you share everything with everyone, all sorts of information can get out—and be seen by people you don't want to see it. The problem is only exacerbated if Facebook shares the information it collects, too.

Facebook has the ability to track not only the personal and contact information you enter on your profile page, but also every single thing you do on the Facebook site, which includes

- Status updates you post

- Other posts you like

- Posts you share

- Comments you make on posts

- The amount of time you spend looking at or reading specific posts

- Your friends (and the amount of time you spend visiting friends' profile pages)

- Any payments you make to purchase apps, products, or services on the Facebook site

- Devices you use to access Facebook—computers, phones, tablets, and so on

Note that Facebook also collects this information from other users who might be reading your posts or interacting with you. Thus, Facebook uses your friends' activities to learn more about you, too.

In addition, Facebook tracks your activity on sites on which you've signed in with your Facebook account. Facebook not only tracks the individual sites you sign into, but also what you do when you're on those sites.

Why does Facebook track all this activity? For a number of reasons.

First, Facebook tracks your activity to decide what posts you see in your News Feed. That's the Top Content model, where your prior interactions determine the future content of your Feed. If you spend more time interacting with posts from a given friend or group, you'll see more posts for that person or group in the future.

Second, Facebook uses the information it gathers to better target the ads you see on its site. This is why you might see an ad for running shoes after you make a post about jogging in your neighborhood. It seems eerily prescient and intrusive, but otherwise you'd see a bunch of random ads instead. (And you'll always see ads, no matter what; that's how Facebook makes money.)

Note that Facebook doesn't sell your personal data to third parties. (That's a good thing.) However, any site you've logged into with your Facebook credentials can access and share your personal data, as can any app or game you use on the Facebook site. (You give them your permission to do so when you agree to use the app—which you probably didn't catch before you clicked.)

Configuring Privacy Options

Facebook lets you configure a variety of options that affect your privacy on its site. You can control who sees the posts you make and the photos you upload, as well as manage the data that Facebook collects about you.

The majority of these privacy options are centralized on the Privacy Shortcuts page. You can configure these options from either the Facebook mobile app or, on your computer, the Facebook website.

Review Important Privacy Settings

You control your main privacy settings from the Privacy Shortcuts screen.

(1) On the Facebook website, click the Quick Help icon on the toolbar; then click Privacy Shortcuts and proceed to step 3. Or...

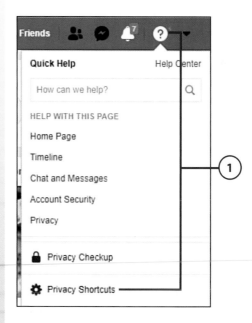

(2) In the Facebook mobile app, tap the More icon, tap to expand the Settings & Privacy section, and then tap Privacy Shortcuts.

(3) The Privacy Shortcuts screen opens. Tap or click Review a Few Important Privacy Settings.

(4) Click or Tap next to begin your privacy checkup.

(5) Tap or click the Privacy button to select who can see your next post.

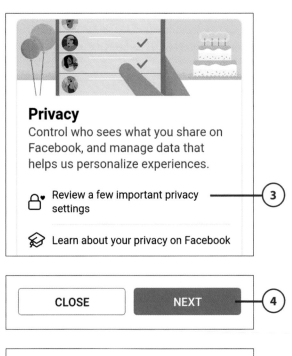

Privacy
Control who sees what you share on Facebook, and manage data that helps us personalize experiences.

Review a few important privacy settings ——————(3)

Learn about your privacy on Facebook

CLOSE	NEXT

(4)

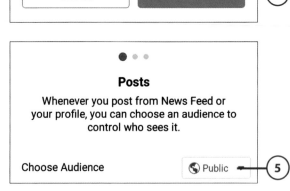

● ● ●

Posts
Whenever you post from News Feed or your profile, you can choose an audience to control who sees it.

Choose Audience   🌐 Public ——(5)

6 Select Public to let everyone on Facebook see the post.

7 Select Friends to make a post visible only to people on your friends list.

8 Select Friends Except and then select specific people or groups who you don't want to see the post.

9 Click See More on your mobile device to view more privacy options. (If necessary on the website, click More.)

10 Select Specific Friends to show this post only to those friends you select.

11 Select Only Me to hide this post from everyone except yourself.

12 Select See All to share this post with a specific list of individuals.

13 In the mobile app, tap Done to return to the Your Next Post screen.

14 Tap or click Next.

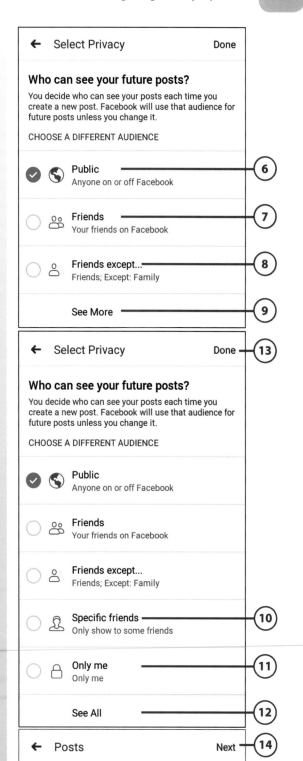

← Select Privacy   Done

Who can see your future posts?
You decide who can see your posts each time you create a new post. Facebook will use that audience for future posts unless you change it.

CHOOSE A DIFFERENT AUDIENCE

✓ 🌐 **Public** ——————————— 6
Anyone on or off Facebook

○ 👥 **Friends** ——————————— 7
Your friends on Facebook

○ 👤 **Friends except...** ——————— 8
Friends; Except: Family

See More ——————————————— 9

← Select Privacy   Done —13

Who can see your future posts?
You decide who can see your posts each time you create a new post. Facebook will use that audience for future posts unless you change it.

CHOOSE A DIFFERENT AUDIENCE

✓ 🌐 **Public**
Anyone on or off Facebook

○ 👥 **Friends**
Your friends on Facebook

○ 👤 **Friends except...**
Friends; Except: Family

○ 👤 **Specific friends** ——————— 10
Only show to some friends

○ 🔒 **Only me** ——————————— 11
Only me

See All ——————————————— 12

← Posts   Next —14

(15) The Your Profile Privacy screen opens. Tap or click the Privacy button next to each contact item to select who can see it—Public, Friends, Only Me, and so on. Select Only Me to hide this information from everyone else on Facebook.

(16) Tap or click Next.

(17) The Your App Privacy screen opens. All the apps and websites you interact with are listed here. To remove any app or websites, tap or click to select it and then tap or click the Remove button.

(18) Tap or click the Privacy button for any app or website to change who can see that item—Public, Friends, and so on. Tap or click Only Me to hide this item from everyone on Facebook.

(19) Tap or click Next.

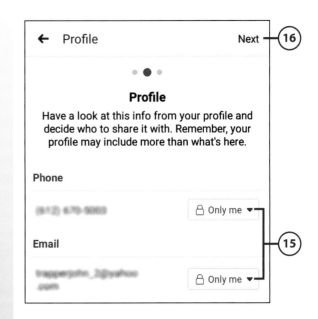

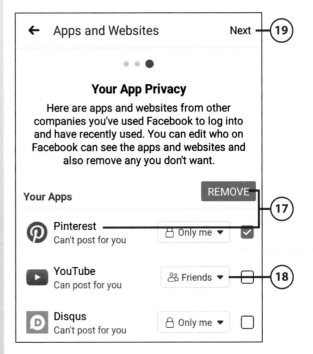

20 Your Privacy Checkup is complete. Tap or click the Close button.

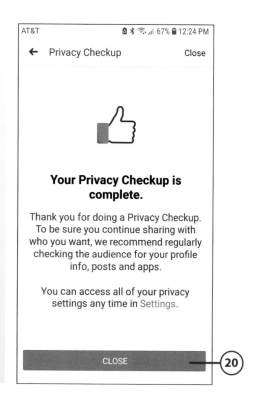

Control Facebook's Face Recognition

Facebook likes to connect people with each other. This is often done via "tagging," where one user can tag ("who are you with?") another user in a status update or photo without asking the other person. When you're tagged, you're connected to that post or photo, whether you want to be or not—which can be an invasion of your privacy.

One of the ways that Facebook encourages tagging is by suggesting people to tag when someone posts a photo. Facebook does this via facial recognition technology; it compares a given photo with the millions of other photos uploaded to its site and tries to match a new face with one it already knows.

So if someone uploads a picture of someone who looks like you, Facebook suggests that you be tagged in that photo. That's fine, unless that's not really you— or if the photo is one you'd rather not be associated with. Fortunately, you can turn off these photo tag suggestions.

It's Not All Good

You Can Still Be Tagged

Just because you turn off Facebook's ability to suggest your name when someone uploads a photo, that doesn't mean you can't be tagged in that photo. The person who uploaded the photo can still manually tag you, even if your name isn't automatically suggested.

(1) From the Privacy Shortcuts screen either in the mobile app or on the Facebook website, tap or click Control Face Recognition.

(2) Facial recognition is enabled by default. To turn it off, click or tap Do You Want Facebook to Be Able to Recognize You in Photos and Videos? and then select No.

Privacy

Control who sees what you share on Facebook, and manage data that helps us personalize experiences.

- Review a few important privacy settings
- Learn about your privacy on Facebook
- Manage your location settings
- Control face recognition ———— **(1)**

← Face Recognition

To recognize whether you're in a photo or video our system compares it with your profile picture, and photos and videos that you're tagged in. This lets us know when you're in other photos and videos so we can create better experiences.
Learn More

Face Recognition

Do you want Facebook to be able to recognize you in photos and videos? ———— **(2)**
Yes

Configuring Account Security Options

Facebook lets you control which personal information is stored on its site and who can see that information.

Review Account Security Settings

Your account security settings are accessible from the Privacy Shortcuts screen both in the mobile app and on the Facebook website.

(1) From the Privacy Shortcuts screen, scroll to the Account Security section.

(2) Tap or click Update Your Personal Information to edit your name, email address, phone number, and Legacy Contact settings.

(3) Tap or click Change Your Password to change your Facebook password.

(4) Tap Get Alerts About Unrecognized Logins to receive a notification when you or someone else tries to log in to your Facebook account from an unfamiliar location or web browser.

(5) Tap Use Two-Factor Authentication to require an extra login code when you log in to your Facebook account from an unrecognized phone or computer.

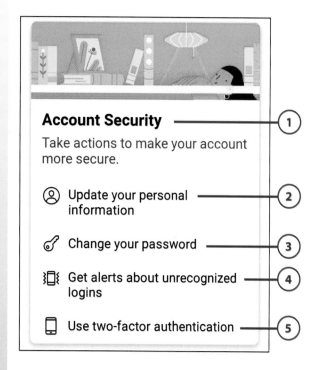

Account Security ——————— (1)

Take actions to make your account more secure.

(2) Update your personal information ————— (2)

⟨ Change your password ——————— (3)

⟩▢⟨ Get alerts about unrecognized ——— (4)
logins

▢ Use two-factor authentication ——— (5)

Configuring Advertising Preferences

Facebook can share the data it collects with a variety of third parties, including advertisers, apps, and websites. This access used to be kept somewhat secretive, but Facebook is now more open about what it shares with whom. You can even tell Facebook not to share selected data, in many cases.

Review Facebook Ad Settings

Facebook collects and analyzes a variety of data that it uses to select which ads from which advertisers you see on its site. If Facebook, for example, thinks that you're married, have a college education, and like Star Trek and HGTV, it shows you ads for products and services that relate to these interests.

You can, however, view what Facebook feeds to its advertisers—and, to a degree, edit this information. You do this from the Privacy Shortcuts screen in either the mobile app or Facebook website.

(1) From the Privacy Shortcuts screen, scroll to the Ad Preferences section.

(2) Tap or click Review Your Ad Preferences.

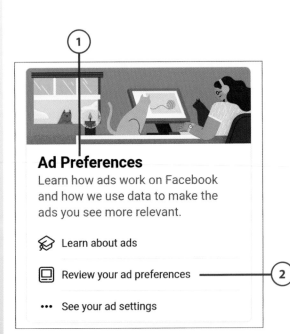

Ad Preferences

Learn how ads work on Facebook and how we use data to make the ads you see more relevant.

🎓 Learn about ads

🖥 Review your ad preferences

••• See your ad settings

(**3**) In the Your Interests section, select a topic to view and edit all the interests you've professed in that area. (Not available in the mobile app.)

(**4**) Tap or click Advertisers to view entities who have served ads to you, or remove ads from a given advertiser.

(**5**) Tap or click Your Information to view specific information Facebook knows about you.

(**6**) Tap or click Ad Settings to view and edit the types of ads that Facebook serves to your News Feed.

(**7**) Tap or click Hide Ad Topics to turn off specific types of ads.

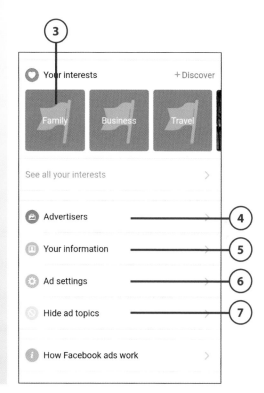

Viewing Your Facebook Information

Facebook collects a lot of information about you but lets you see what it's collected. (You'll be surprised how much it collects!)

Access and Manage Your Information

You can view and manage the data Facebook collects about you from the Privacy Shortcuts screen in either the mobile app or the Facebook website.

(1) From the Privacy Shortcuts screen, scroll to the Your Facebook Information section.

(2) Tap or click Access Your Information to view your posts, photos and videos, comments, likes and reactions, friends, people you're following and those who are following you, messages, groups, events, profile information, pages, Marketplace activity, payment history, saved items, places you've created, apps and websites you log into using Facebook, ad-related info, information associated with your Facebook account, search history, location history, calls and messages, and security and login information.

(3) Tap or click See Your Activity Log to view a log of your recent Facebook activity.

(4) Tap or click Manage Your Information to edit your personal information.

(5) Tap or click Delete Your Account and Information to delete your Facebook account.

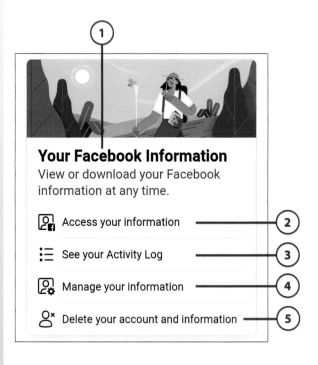

Your Facebook Information

View or download your Facebook information at any time.

Access your information   — **(2)**

See your Activity Log   — **(3)**

Manage your information   — **(4)**

Delete your account and information   — **(5)**

10

Following Interesting People on Twitter

Twitter is different from Facebook in that it's not a social network; it's a *microblogging service*. That means it's like Facebook but without the group social interaction. The focus is on relatively short (280-character) messages called tweets, which are shared with a user's followers.

As such, Twitter is immensely popular with younger users, but less so among older users, who value the more social nature of Facebook and Pinterest. Although there aren't a whole lot of people 50+ who actively tweet, there are quite a few who join Twitter to follow the postings of their 20- and 30-something family members or of their favorite politicians and celebrities.

Signing Up and Signing On

Like most other social media, Twitter is free. If you want to follow other users' tweets, as well as tweet yourself, you need to create an account.

You access Twitter—and create your new account—from Twitter's home page on the web or the Twitter mobile app.

Mobile App

The Twitter app is available for Android, iOS (Apple), and Windows Phone devices. Download the app, for free, from your device's app store. (I use the Android app for the examples in this chapter.)

Create and Log In To Your Account—from the Twitter App

Twitter ①

Most people use Twitter on their mobile phones. We look first at how to join up with the Twitter app.

① Launch the Twitter app on your phone or tablet.

② To create a new account, enter your first name, last name, email address, and desired password; then tap Agree & Join. Follow the onscreen instructions to complete your new account registration.

③ Tap Sign In to sign in to an existing account. You need to enter either your username, phone number, or email address—plus password, of course—when prompted.

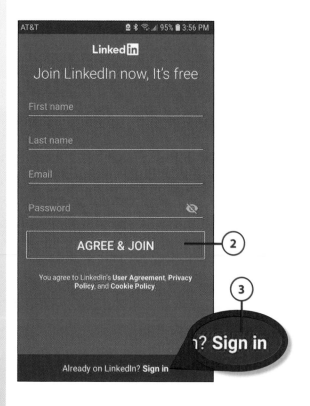

Create and Log In To Your Account—on the Web

You can also log in to and use Twitter on your desktop or notebook computer. All you need is your web browser.

1 In your web browser, go to www.twitter.com. Click the Sign Up button and follow the onscreen instructions to create a new account. You need to enter your name, phone number or email address, and desired password.

2 Click one of the Log In buttons and follow the onscreen instructions to sign in to an existing account. You need to enter either your email address, phone number, or username, along with your password.

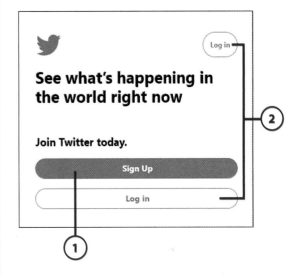

Navigating Twitter

Both the Twitter website and mobile app are organized into sections, which are accessible via individual tabs.

Tweeting

Learn more about creating your own tweets in Chapter 11, "Tweeting and Retweeting on Twitter."

Navigate the Twitter App

Most people access Twitter from their mobile phones. This section gives you a tour of Twitter's mobile app.

① Tap Home to view the Home timeline of tweets from the people you follow. Scroll down the screen to view additional tweets.

② Tap your profile picture to display shortcuts and settings, including who you're following (Following) and who is following you (Followers).

③ Tap the Tweet button to create a new tweet of your own.

④ Tap Search to view trending topics and search for topics on Twitter.

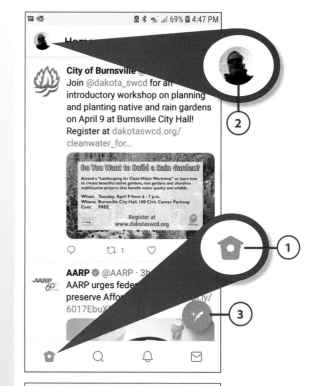

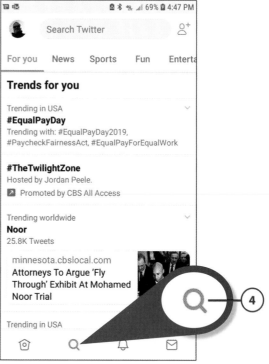

(5) Tap Notifications to view your interactions with other Twitter users.

(6) Tap Messages to view private messages from other users.

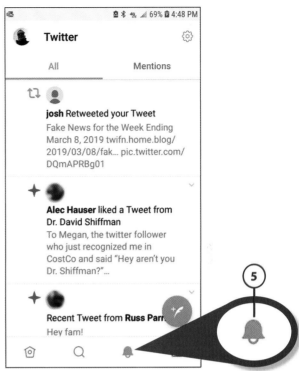

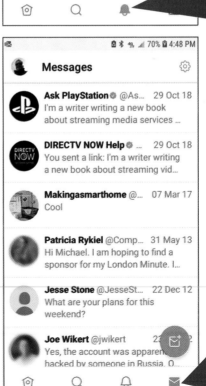

Navigate the Twitter Website

You can also access Twitter from your notebook or desktop computer. Use your web browser to go to www.twitter.com and noodle around from there.

1. Click Home to view the Home timeline of tweets from the people you follow. Scroll down the screen to view additional tweets.

2. Click your name in the top-right corner to view shortcuts and settings, including who you're following (Following) and who is following you (Followers).

3. Click within the search box to search for specific people or topics.

4. Click the Tweet button to create a new tweet.

5. Click the hashtag (#) icon to view trending topics.

6. Click Notifications to view your interactions with other Twitter users.

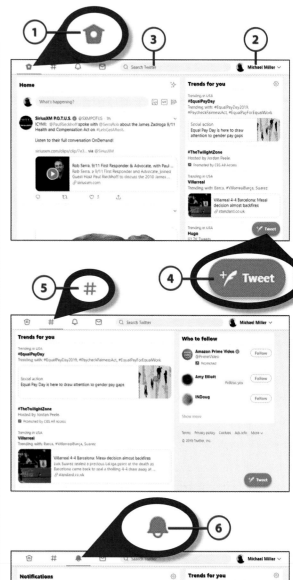

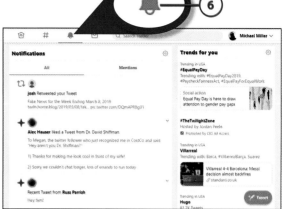

7 Click Messages to view private messages from other users.

Finding Tweeters to Follow

Tweets from users you follow appear in your Home timeline. You can follow any Twitter user you want.

Unlike Facebook, where friends and connections have to be mutually approved, you don't have to be approved to view another user's tweets. So if you want to follow Paul McCartney (@PaulMcCartney) or CNN (@CNN) or just your neighbor down the street, you can do so without having to ask permission.

(There are two exceptions to this. First, a user can "protect" their tweets, requiring you to receive permission to follow them. Second, a user can specifically block you as a follower; any user can block any other user, which helps to cut down on online stalking.)

@name

Users on Twitter are identified by a username preceded by an ampersand (@). So, for example, my username is molehillgroup, which translates into my Twitter "handle" of @molehillgroup.

Accept Twitter's Recommendations

There are several ways to find people to follow on Twitter. One approach is to accept the recommendations that Twitter makes based on your past activities and interests.

1. In the mobile app, tap the Search icon to display the search page.

2. Tap the Connect or tool gear icon in the top-right corner.

3. Scroll down to view a list of recommendations, typically friends of people or organizations you already follow.

4. Tap the Follow button to follow a given user. *Or…*

5. Tap the user's name to view that member's profile page.

On the Website

On the Twitter website, you find new people to follow by clicking the hashtag (#) icon to display the Explore page. On that page, go to the Who to Follow pane to view Twitter's suggestions; click Show More to view even more. Click Follow to follow any given account.

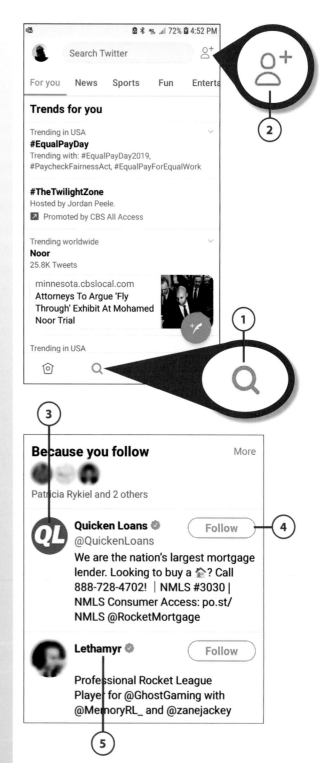

Follow Your Contacts

You can follow people who are in your phone's contacts list. Twitter searches your phone for contacts who are already members of the service.

(1) In the mobile app, tap the Search icon to display the search page.

(2) Tap the Connect icon in the top-right corner.

(3) In the Find Friends section, tap the Get Started button.

(4) Tap Sync Contacts. (If prompted to allow Twitter access to your contacts, tap Allow.)

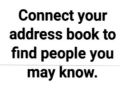

Find friends

See who you already know on Twitter. Don't worry, you'll choose who to follow.

Get started —— (3)

Connect your address book to find people you may know.

Sync contacts —— (4)

5 Twitter displays contacts who are also on Twitter. Tap the Follow button to follow any given individual.

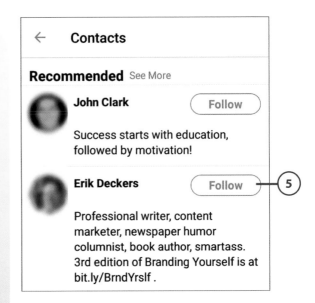

Search for People and Organizations to Follow

Twitter also lets you search for specific members and organizations to follow.

1 In the mobile app or on the website, tap the Search icon or click within the search box.

2 Enter the name of the person or organization you want to follow.

3 Twitter displays a list of matching members. Tap a name to go to that member's profile page.

4 Tap Follow to follow this member.

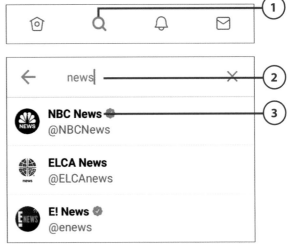

Unfollow a User

At any time, you can opt to no longer follow a particular tweeter. This act is called unfollowing.

1. From anywhere in the Twitter app or on the Twitter website, click or tap a member's name to go to that profile page.

2. Click or tap the Following button to unfollow this person.

Viewing Your Twitter Feed

When you select other users to follow, you receive all their tweets in Twitter's Home timeline.

View Tweets

A tweet is a post to the Twitter service. The text in each tweet must be 280 characters or less in length. Tweets can include not only text but also images, videos, and links to other web pages.

1. Tap or click the Home icon to view the tweets in your timeline.

2. Tweets are listed in reverse chronological order, with the newest tweets at the top. The name of the tweeter and how long ago the tweet was made are listed at the top of each tweet. Scroll down the page to view older tweets.

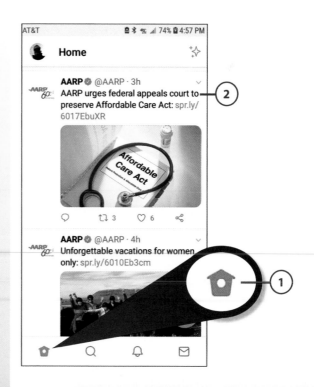

3 To view the profile summary for a given person or organization, tap or click that user's name or @ name within the tweet.

4 To "like" a tweet, tap or click the Like (heart) icon.

5 To view other tweets on a high-lighted topic, tap or click the hashtag (#topic) within the tweet. (Not all tweets include hashtags.)

6 To view a web page linked to within a tweet, tap or click the embedded URL.

3

4

5

6

7 Photos are embedded within tweets, but at a limited height. To view the full picture, tap or click it.

Reply to a Tweet

You can respond to any tweet you read. All you have to do is click the Reply button in the original tweet. Your reply is sent as a tweet back to the original sender.

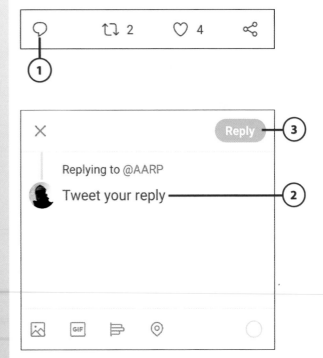

1 Tap or click the Reply icon for the tweet to which you want to reply. This opens a new screen (mobile) or panel (website).

2 The sender's name appears in the reply box, preceded by the @ sign. Enter your reply (280 characters max, of course) into the reply box.

3 Tap or click Reply to send the reply as a tweet.

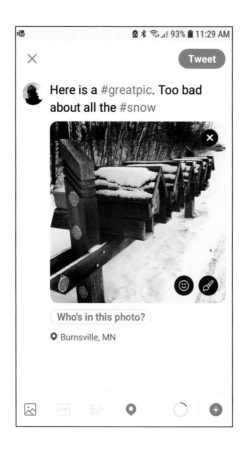

In this chapter, you learn how to create your own tweets—and retweet other tweets you like.

→ Posting Your Own Tweets
→ Retweeting Tweets from Others

11

Tweeting and Retweeting on Twitter

Most people use Twitter to keep up with what's going on by reading tweets posted by others. But you can also create your own tweets—and retweet tweets you like from others.

Posting Your Own Tweets

Posting a message to Twitter is called *tweeting*. The posts you make are called *tweets*.

You can tweet from your computer, using your web browser to access the Twitter site. You also can tweet from your mobile phone or tablet, using Twitter's mobile app.

Post a Tweet from the Twitter Website

Tweets are limited to 280 characters of text. (You can also post photos and videos, which are covered later in this chapter.) Because of the 280-character limitation, tweets do not have to conform to proper grammar, spelling, and sentence structure—and, in fact, seldom do. It is common to abbreviate longer words, use familiar acronyms, substitute single letters and numbers for whole words, and refrain from all punctuation. (For example, you might shorten the sentence "I'll see you on Friday" to read "CU Fri.")

1. From anywhere on the Twitter website, click the floating Tweet button. This displays the Compose New Tweet panel.

2. Type your message into the What's Happening? box. Remember that a tweet can be no more than 280 characters in length.

3. When you're ready, click the Tweet button.

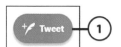

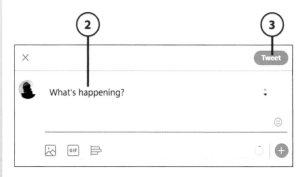

Web Links

To include a link to another website in your tweet, simply type the URL as part of your message. You may use a link-shortening service, such as bit.ly (www.bit.ly), to create shorter URLs to fit within Twitter's 280-character limit.

Post a Tweet from the Mobile App

Tweeting from your smartphone or tablet is just as easy as tweeting from your computer.

(**1**) From any screen in the mobile app, tap the Tweet button. You see the Compose New Tweet screen.

(**2**) Use your phone's onscreen keyboard to type your message into the What's Happening? box. Remember that a tweet can be no more than 280 characters in length.

(**3**) Tap the Tweet button.

Mention Other Users

When you mention other Twitter users in your tweets, their names become clickable by anyone viewing the tweets. Clicking a referenced name displays that user's Twitter profile summary.

(**1**) Start a new tweet as normal.

(**2**) Type an ampersand (@) before the user's name, like this: **@username**.

(**3**) As you type, Twitter lists matching users. Select a user from the list or finish typing.

(**4**) Tap or click the Tweet button to post the tweet.

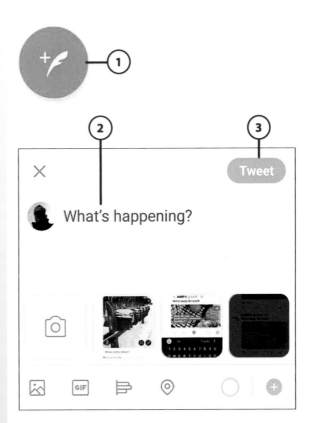

Use Hashtags

When you add a hash character (#) before a specific word in a tweet, that word gets referenced by Twitter as a kind of keyword, or hashtag, and that word becomes clickable by anyone viewing the tweet. Clicking a hashtag in a tweet displays a list of the most recent tweets that include the same hashtag.

1. Start a new tweet as normal.

2. Type a hash character or pound sign (#) before the word you want to reference, like this: **#keyword**.

3. As you type, matching hashtags are listed. Select a hashtag from the list or finish typing.

4. Tap or click the Tweet button to post the tweet.

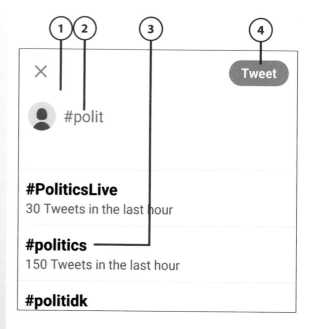

>>>*Go Further*

HASHTAGS

A *hashtag* is a word or phrase (with no spaces) in a tweet that is preceded by the hash or pound character, like this: **#hashtag**. Hashtags function much like keywords by helping other users find relevant tweets when searching for a particular topic. A hashtag within a tweet is clickable; clicking a hashtag displays a list of the most recent tweets that include that word.

You can use hashtags to find tweets related to a given topic. Hashtags are particularly valuable when looking for information on a current or trending topic.

For this reason, it's common (and expected) for tweets to include one or more hashtags. The more you can use hashtags to connect to popular and trending topics, the better.

Tweet a Picture or Video from Your Phone

Tweets started out as text-only posts, but now Twitter lets you embed images and videos in your tweets.

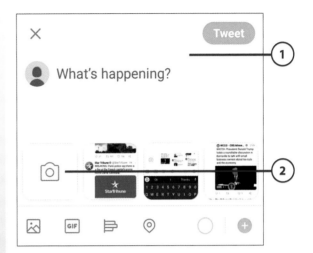

(1) Start a new tweet as you normally would.

(2) To take a photo in the mobile app, tap the camera icon.

(3) You see your phone's camera screen; tap to take a picture or tap and hold to take a video.

(4) Enter the text of your tweet into the What's Happening? box.

(5) Tap the Tweet button to post the tweet.

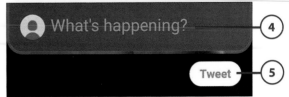

Tweet a Stored Photo

You can also tweet photos stored on your phone or computer.

1. Begin a new tweet as normal.

2. Click or tap the Picture icon.

3. On your computer, you see the Open dialog box. Navigate to the photo or video you want to add and then click the Open button. *Or...*

4. In the mobile app, you see the Gallery screen. Navigate to and select the item you want, and then tap Done.

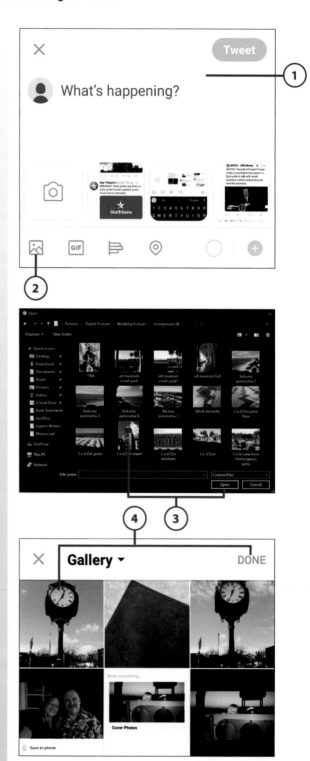

5 The photo or video is added to your tweet. Add a comment (280 characters or fewer) if you want.

6 Tap or click Tweet to post the tweet to Twitter.

Add Your Location to a Tweet

Twitter also lets you add your location to a tweet. This is especially useful if you're tweeting from your mobile phone.

1 Start a new tweet as you normally would.

2 Tap or click the Tag Location button.

(3) Select one of the suggested locations. *Or…*

(4) Enter your current location into the Search Locations box.

(5) The location is added to your tweet. Finish the tweet as necessary and then tap or click the Tweet button.

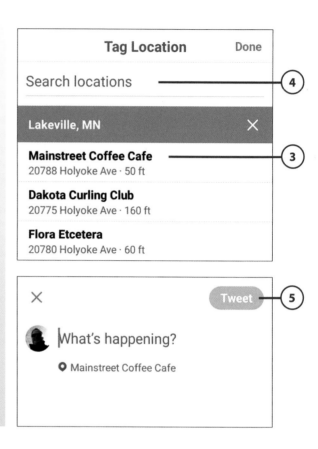

Retweeting Tweets from Others

Ofttimes you'll see a tweet from some person or organization in your feed that you'd like to share with your friends. You do this by *retweeting* the original tweet. (The new tweet you send is called a *retweet*.) You can retweet from either the Twitter website or mobile app.

Retweet from the Website

(1) From the Twitter home page, click the Retweet icon for the tweet you want to share.

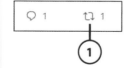

(2) Select Retweet to retweet without additional comment. *Or…*

(3) Select Retweet with Comment to
add a comment.

(4) Enter your comments (optional)
into the Add a Comment box.

(5) Click the Retweet button.

Retweet from the Mobile App

(1) Tap the Retweet icon for the
tweet you want to retweet.

(2) Tap Retweet to retweet the tweet
without comment. *Or…*

(3) Tap Retweet with Comment
to add a comment before
retweeting.

(4) If you clicked Retweet with
Comment, add your comments
into the Add a Comment box.

(5) Tap Retweet when done.

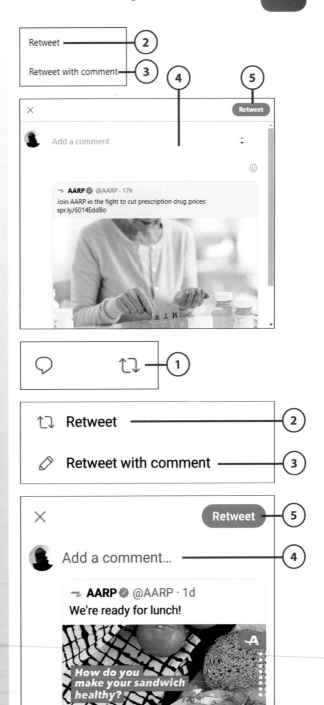

In this chapter, you learn about Pinterest, the visual social network.

→ Getting to Know Pinterest
→ Viewing and Saving Pins
→ Saving Pins from the Web
→ Creating New Boards

Pinning and Repinning on Pinterest

Pinterest (www.pinterest.com) is a social network with particular appeal to women—although there are a growing number of male users, too.

Getting to Know Pinterest

Unlike Facebook, which lets you post text-based status updates, Pinterest is all about images. The site consists of a collection of boards, like virtual corkboards, that people use to share pictures they find interesting. The items you share are called *pins*, and you save these pins to your own boards. People who follow you see your pins in their feeds—and you see their pins in yours.

Pins on Pinterest are more than just pretty pictures, however. When you click or tap a pin, it links back to the web page for that particular image. This way you can read more information about an image—or get a detailed recipe or set of instructions for a home improvement project.

You can save images of anything—clothing, furniture, recipes, do-it-yourself (DIY) projects, and the like. Your Pinterest friends can then save your pins to their boards—and on and on. You can also *like* other people's pins and save their items to your boards, thus repeating the original pin. It's a visual way to share things you like online.

A Pinterest board becomes a place where you can create and share collections of those things you like or find interesting. You can have up to as many 500 boards, organized by category or topic.

Signing Up for Pinterest

Joining Pinterest is free; in fact, you can sign up using your Facebook username and password (or with your email address, of course). To sign up on your computer, point your web browser to www.pinterest.com, enter your email address, age, and desired password, and then click Continue. To sign up from your phone or tablet, launch the Pinterest mobile app (available for free from your device's app store), enter your email address, and tap Continue or Next. Follow the onscreen instructions from there.

Navigate the Pinterest Website

If you're visiting Pinterest from your desktop or laptop computer, it's relatively easy to get around the Pinterest website. After you've logged on, it's a simple matter of displaying and viewing pins and boards.

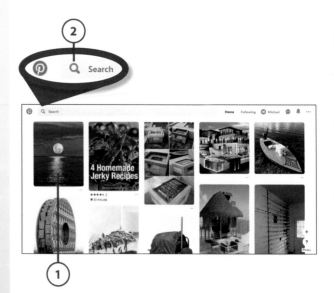

(1) When you first log in to Pinterest, you see the Home page. Pins from boards and users you follow are displayed here; scroll down to view older pins.

(2) Search for specific pins or users by entering your query into the Search box at the top of the page.

3. Click your profile icon or picture to view your own boards and pins.

4. Click the Notifications button to view notifications from Pinterest and information about which of your pins have been saved by others.

5. Click the Pinterest or Home button to return to the home page from any other page of the site.

Navigate the Pinterest App

More and more people are using Pinterest on their smartphones and tablets using Pinterest's mobile app. It's as easy to navigate as the website is.

1. When you launch Pinterest's mobile app, you see the Home screen. Pins from boards and users you follow are displayed here; scroll down to view older pins.

2. Search for specific pins or users by entering your query into the Search box at the top of the page.

3. Tap the Saved (profile) icon at the bottom right to view all the boards and pins you've saved.

4. Tap the Notifications icon to view notifications from Pinterest and information about which of your pins have been saved by others.

5. Tap the Home button to return to the home page from any other page of the site.

Viewing and Saving Pins

All items pinned on Pinterest have the same overall format. You can view more information about any pin, as well as the person who pinned it. You can also "repin" a pin to one of your own boards.

View a Pin on the Pinterest Website

Pins from people and boards you follow are displayed in the visual feed on your Pinterest home page. What options you have differ slightly between the website and the mobile app.

1. On the Pinterest website, mouse over the image to display the action buttons.

2. Click the Share button to share this pin to Facebook or Twitter, or to email the pin's URL to a friend.

3. Click the Save button to save this button to one of your boards.

4. Click the pin's image to view this item's details page.

5. Click the user's name to view other boards and pins from this user.

6. Click the Visit button (or just click the image itself) to view the website where the image was originally found.

7. Click Comments to comment on this pin, and then enter your text into the Add a Comment box.

8. Click the Save button to save this pin to one of your boards.

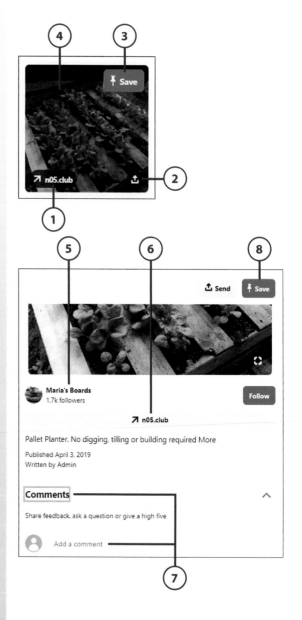

View a Pin in the Mobile App

Viewing a pin is slightly different when you're using Pinterest's mobile app, and the layout varies a tad between the Android and the iOS apps. I've used the iOS version for these steps.

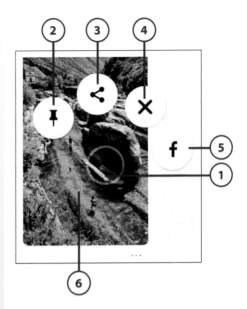

1. Press and hold the pin to display the action buttons.

2. Tap the Save (pin) icon to save this pin to one of your boards.

3. Tap the Share icon to share this pin with other users, to Facebook or Twitter, or via email.

4. Tap the X to hide this pin—and display fewer like this one.

5. Tap the Facebook icon to share this pin in a Facebook post.

6. Tap the pin's image to view this item's details page.

7. Tap the Visit or Read It or Make It button, or tap the image itself, to view the website where the image was originally found.

8. Tap the user's name to view other pins and boards from this user on their profile page.

9. Tap the name of the user's board to display all the pins in this particular board.

10. Click the Save button to save this pin to one of your boards.

Save a Pin

Some people say that Pinterest is a little like a refrigerator covered with magnets holding up tons of photos and drawings. You can find lots of interesting items pinned from other users—and then save them to your boards.

(1) On the Pinterest website, mouse over the item you want to save to display the action buttons.

(2) Pull down the board list to select which board to save to.

(3) Click Save.

(4) In the mobile app, press and hold the pinned image to display the action buttons.

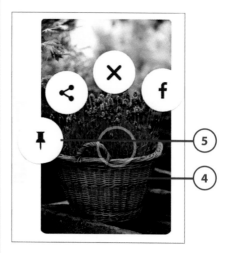

(5) Tap the Save (pin) icon.

(6) Accept the existing description or enter your own.

(7) Tap the board to which you want to pin this item. The item is saved to that board.

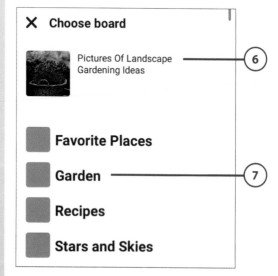

Saving Pins from the Web

In addition to saving items you find on the Pinterest site, you can also pin images you find on the web—using either your computer or mobile phone.

Save a Pin from a Web Page on Your Computer

To pin an image you find on a web page, all you need is that page's web address.

1. From any page on the Pinterest website, click the + button in the lower-right corner.

2. Click Create a Pin.

3. On the next page, click Save from Site.

4. Enter the web address (URL) of the web page that contains the image you want to save, and then press the Enter key on your computer keyboard or click the right arrow.

5. Pinterest displays all images found on the selected web page. Click the image you want to pin.

6. Click Add to Pin.

7. Enter a title for this pin.

8. Enter a short (500 characters or fewer) text description of this image.

9. Pull down the Choose a Board list and select the board to which you want to save this image, or click Create Board to pin the image to a new board.

10. Click Save.

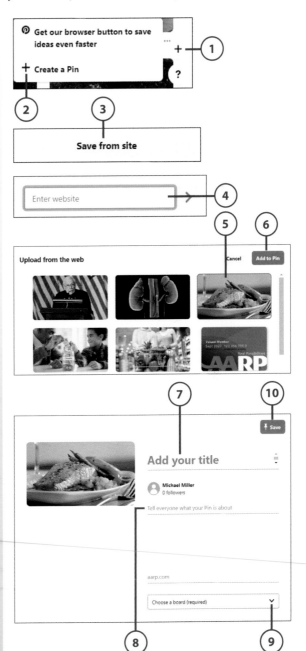

(11) The image is saved to the selected board. Click Close to return to Pinterest, or click See It Now to view the pin.

It's Not All Good

Not Always Welcome

Some websites don't want people to pin their images, so they code their pages to prohibit pinning. If you try to pin from one of these pages, you get a message that no pinnable images have been found. If you happen to pin an image that some entity owns and doesn't want you to pin, that entity can ask Pinterest to take down the pin. (Legally, Pinterest says it's not responsible for any copyright claims for items pinned to its site.)

>>>Go Further
PIN IT FROM YOUR BROWSER

It's even easier to pin an image from a web page if you install Pinterest's Browser Button in your web browser. To do this, click the + button and select Get Our Browser Button to Save Ideas Even Faster. Follow the onscreen instructions to install the Pin It button in your browser's toolbar.

When you next visit a web page that you'd like to pin from, click the Pinterest button in your browser. You'll see images from this web page; click the image you want to save and proceed from there.

Save a Pin from a Web Page on Your Phone

It's easy to save images you find on web pages when you're using Pinterest on your mobile phone or tablet.

1. Use your phone's web browser to open the page that contains the image you want to save.

2. If you're using the Chrome browser, tap the More or Menu button in your browser. Otherwise, proceed to step 3.

3. Tap Share.

4. Tap the Pinterest icon.

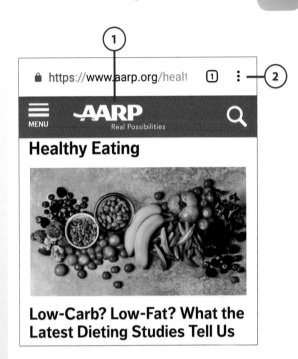

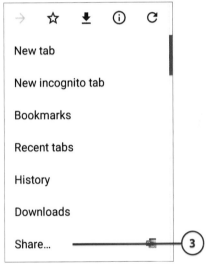

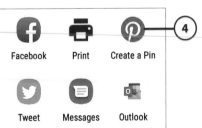

5 You see all images found on the selected web page. Tap the image you want to pin.

6 Accept, edit, or enter a new text description for this image.

7 Select the board to which you want to save this image, or tap Create Board to pin the image to a new board. The image is now saved to that board.

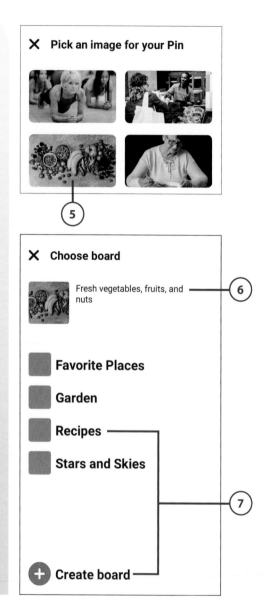

Creating New Boards

Pinterest lets you create any number of boards, each dedicated to specific topics. If you're into quilting, you can create a Quilting board; if you're into radio-controlled airplanes, you can create an RC Airplanes board with pictures of your favorite craft.

Create a Board

When you first join Pinterest, you're prompted to create boards to match your personal tastes. You can, however, create new boards at any time—up to 500 in total, which should be plenty.

1. Click the profile or Saved icon to display your profile page.

2. On the Pinterest website, click the + icon, and then click Create Board. Proceed to step 5.

3. In the mobile app, tap the + icon on your profile page.

4. Tap Board (Android) or Create Board (iOS).

5. Enter the name for this board into the Name (website) or Board Name (mobile app) box.

6. Select Secret (website) or Keep Board Secret (mobile app) if you want to make this board private, so only you can see it.

7. Click or tap the Create button.

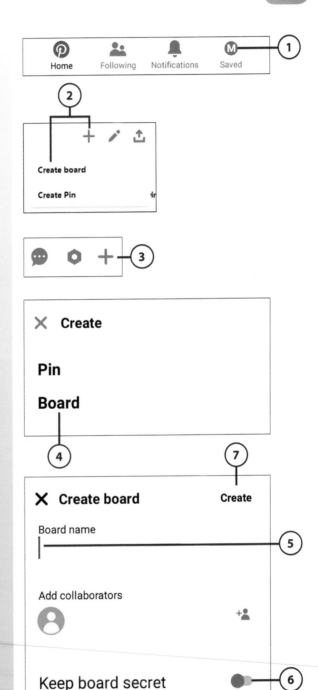

View Your Boards and Pins

You can view all your boards and pins from your personal page on Pinterest.

1. Click or tap the profile or Saved icon.

2. See your boards by clicking or tapping the Boards tab.

3. See your individual pins by clicking or tapping the Pins tab.

4. View suggested pins for your boards by clicking or tapping Topics.

5. Click or tap Followers to display the people following your pins.

6. See the users and boards that you are following by clicking or tapping Following.

7. View the items pinned to a given board by clicking or tapping that board.

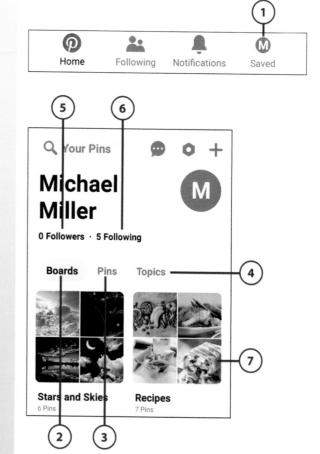

In this chapter, you learn how to find pins, boards, and people on Pinterest.

→ Browsing and Searching for Pins
→ Searching for People and Boards

Finding Other Users and Boards to Follow on Pinterest

How do you find items to save on Pinterest? It's a matter of searching or browsing for specific types of items—and for other pinners to follow.

Browsing and Searching for Pins

With more than 175 billion pins from more than 250 million users around the globe, there's a lot of interesting content to find on Pinterest. How do you sort through all those pins to find the ones you want to save?

Browse via Category

Pinterest organizes its pins into a relative handful of major categories. You can browse through the categories to find the most popular pins of a given type. This section shows you how to do this in Pinterest's mobile app. (The process is similar on the Pinterest website.)

1. Tap the search box to display trending and recommended categories.

2. In the Ideas for You section, tap a topic to view pins of a given type.

3. Pinterest displays suggested pins. Scroll down to view more.

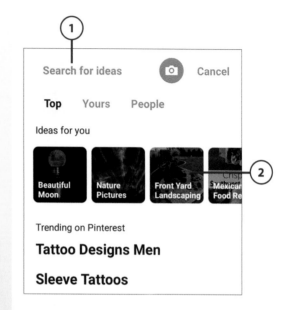

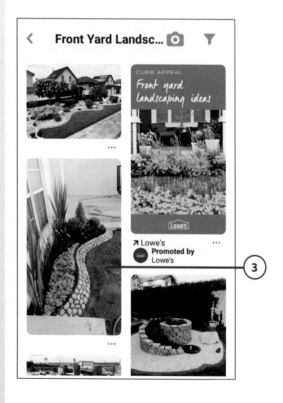

Search by Keyword

You can search for pins of a certain type by entering one or more keywords that describe what you're looking for.

1. Tap within the search box to display the Search for Ideas screen.
2. Enter one or more keywords into the Search for Ideas box.
3. As you type, Pinterest displays suggested searches. If one of these is what you're looking for, tap it.
4. Otherwise, continue entering your query and then tap the Enter or Search key on your device's onscreen keyboard.
5. Pinterest displays pins that match your query. You can fine-tune your search by selecting one of the filters displayed at the top of the search results page.

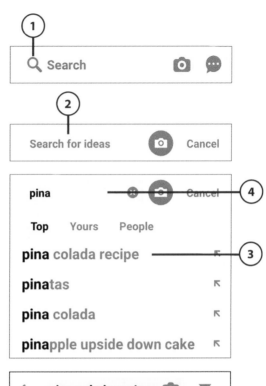

Searching for People and Boards

Pinterest lets you search for boards about a given topic, which you can then follow. You also can search for individual users—and follow them, too. (Pins from any board or user you follow appear in the feed on your Pinterest home page.)

Find and Follow Interesting Boards

Just as you can search for individual pins, you also can search for boards full of pins in which you might be interested.

1. Begin a search as described in the "Search by Keyword" task.

2. When you come to the screen of search results, tap the Filter icon.

3. In the Filter By section, tap Boards.

4. You see boards that match your query. Tap a board to view all the pins saved to that board. Or...

5. Tap the Follow button to follow all pins saved to that board.

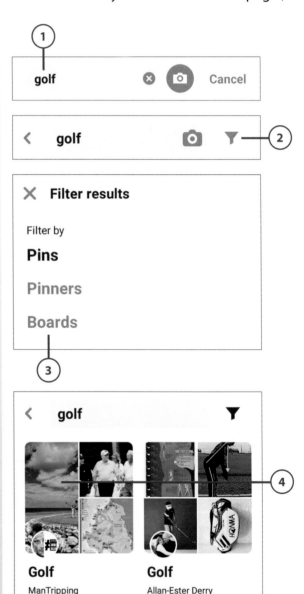

Find Other Users to Follow

Although you can search for individual users by name or by keyword from the Pinterest Search box (just select Pinners or People after tapping the Filter icon), a better approach is to find a pin you like and then click through to learn more about the person who pinned that item. You can then opt to follow that person or specific boards created by that person. (Following a person means that all that person's new pins display on your Pinterest home page.)

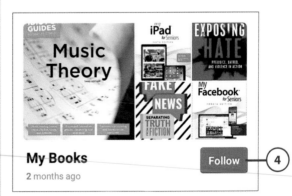

(1) When you find a pin you like, click or tap the pin to view its detail screen.

(2) Click or tap the name of the person who saved it to see that person's profile page.

(3) Click or tap the Follow button to follow all of this person's pins.

(4) Alternatively, if you want to follow pins to only one of this person's boards, scroll down to view all of this person's boards and tap or click the Follow button for the board you want to follow.

Unfollow a Board

Over time, you may find that some boards you follow aren't quite as interesting as you once thought. Fortunately, you can opt to unfollow any board at any time.

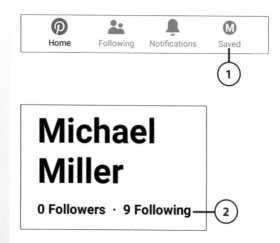

1. Click or tap the Saved (profile) icon to display your personal page.

2. Click or tap Following to display all the people and boards you follow.

3. Click or tap Boards to display the boards you follow.

4. Find the board you no longer want to follow, and then click or tap the Unfollow button.

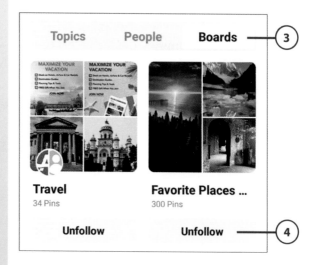

>>>*Go Further*

FOR WOMEN—AND MEN

As we've discussed, Pinterest is particularly appealing to women—more so than any other social network today. Maybe it's the visual nature of Pinterest. Maybe it's because women jumped on the bandwagon first, and that encouraged even more women to join.

Whatever the reasons, Pinterest has a huge following among women of all ages. Women use Pinterest to pin the latest fashions, recipes, DIY and craft projects, you name it. My wife uses it to find recipes for the family meals. My stepdaughter uses it for gift and party ideas for her kids (my grandkids). My friend's wife actually hosts Pinterest craft nights at her church, with fun crafts found on the Pinterest site. You get the idea.

That's not to say that Pinterest is only a female thing. It's not. More and more men are joining Pinterest and pinning items of interest to them. Some of my friends have Pinterest boards for classic automobiles, baseball cards, favorite golf courses, and various other sports and hobbies (including DIY projects, of course—that topic definitely crosses genders). Personally, I've played drums for the past half century, so I have boards devoted to famous drummers, cool drum sets, and musicians in general.

In short, you can use Pinterest to follow anything in which you have an interest. It doesn't matter whether you're male or female, what age you are, or how much money you make. Pinterest is a social network for anyone and everyone.

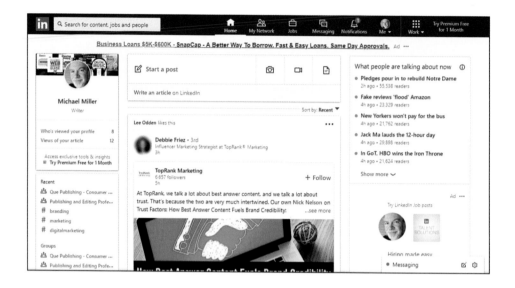

In this chapter, you learn how to create an effective profile for professional networking on the LinkedIn social network.

→ Signing Up and Logging In
→ Creating an Effective Profile

14

Fine-Tuning Your Professional Profile on LinkedIn

LinkedIn is different from Facebook and most other social media, in that it has a distinct focus on business. Businesses use LinkedIn to find potential employees; job hunters use LinkedIn to look for potential employers; and business professionals use LinkedIn to keep in touch with others in their professions.

Even if you're not currently in the job market, LinkedIn is a great way to network with other people in your industry, and to keep tabs on what former co-workers are up to. It's very much a business networking site, using social networking functionality.

Signing Up and Logging In

The basic LinkedIn membership is free; anyone can join. LinkedIn also offers a variety of Premium memberships, from $29.99 to $99.95 per month, designed specifically for serious job hunters, business networkers, and sales professionals. For most people, however, the free membership is the way to go.

Although LinkedIn has a mobile app (available for both Android and Apple devices), most businesspeople access the LinkedIn website via their desktop or laptop computers. Although this chapter focuses on the LinkedIn website, know that you can do most all of these operations in the LinkedIn app.

Create a New Account

When you create your LinkedIn account, you're prompted to enter some basic information, including your job status. You need to do this to create your account, but you can come back later to edit this or enter additional information.

(1) In your web browser, go to www. linkedin.com and click Join Now.

(2) Enter your email address into the Email box.

(3) Enter your desired password into the Password box.

(4) Click Agree & Join.

(5) Enter your first name and last name into the respective boxes.

(6) Click Continue.

(7) Pull down the Country list and select your country, if you're not in the United States.

(8) Enter your ZIP Code into the Zip Code box.

(9) Click Next.

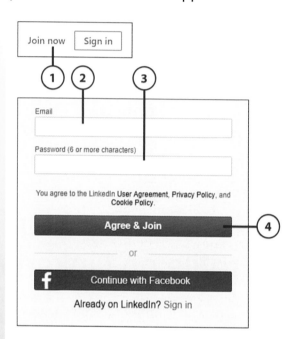

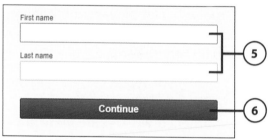

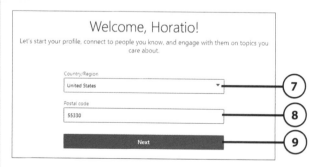

(10) If you're a student (which you probably aren't), click I'm a Student. Otherwise, ignore this.

(11) Enter your current job title into the Most Recent Job Title box.

(12) Enter the name of your employer into the Most Recent Company box. (If the name of your company appears in the drop-down list, click it.)

(13) If the box expands, pull down the Industry list and select the industry that you're in.

(14) Click Continue. You're prompted to verify your email address. You receive a code via email; enter that code, click Agree & Confirm, and follow the onscreen directions to complete your membership.

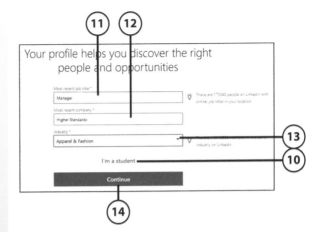

Sign In to Your Account

Once you've created your LinkedIn account, signing in is a quick and easy process.

(1) In your web browser, go to www. linkedin.com and click Sign In.

(2) Enter your email address into the Email box.

(3) Enter your password into the Password box.

(4) Click Sign In. The LinkedIn home page displays.

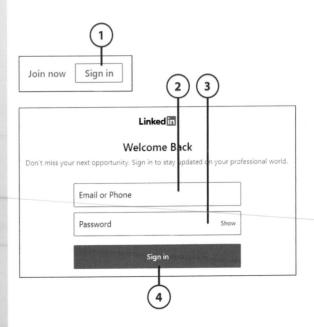

Creating an Effective Profile

Every LinkedIn member has a personal profile page. This profile page is what other LinkedIn users see when they search for you on the site; it's where you make your initial impression to the people you want to make contact with— including potential employers.

Your LinkedIn profile is kind of like a mini-resume, containing important personal and professional information. It's also fully customizable; you can select which content others see.

Your profile page can include any or all of the following sections:

- **Intro:** This opening section is an overview of your personal information, including name, location, current title, past positions, and education. It functions as an online business card—a quick glance at your experience and qualifications.

- **Highlights:** When someone else is viewing your profile, this section shows how many mutual connections you have and whether you both studied at the same school(s).

- **Contact Info:** Includes links to your personal website or blog, your public email address and phone number, and other contact information.

- **Activity:** Displays your most recent activity on the LinkedIn site.

- **Experience:** A listing of your current and previous employment positions, as well as your educational and volunteer experiences, sorted in reverse chronological order.

- **Skills & Endorsements:** Specific professional skills you possess, as well as endorsements from other users.

- **Recommendations:** Any recommendations you've received or given to others.

- **Interests:** Companies and groups that you're following.

Edit Your Intro

Because your profile page serves as your de facto resume on the LinkedIn site, you want to control the information you display to others. The first thing visitors to your profile page see is the Intro section, so that's what you should edit first.

(1) On the LinkedIn menu bar, click the profile picture ("Me") or icon and select View Profile. This displays your profile page.

(2) The Intro section is at the top of the page and contains any information you entered when you signed up for your LinkedIn account. Click the Edit (pencil) icon to display the Edit Intro pop-up.

(3) Add or edit the desired information. Your Intro can include your first and last name, headline, current position, education (typically college attended), country, ZIP Code, locations within your area (other cities or towns in a metro), industry, and summary of your work experience.

(4) Click the Add New Education or Add New Position links to add new education or work information.

(5) Click the Save button.

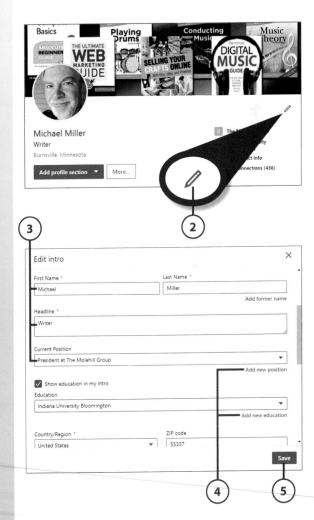

Write Well

Write your summary in complete sentences using proper grammar and punctuation. Appearances matter to future employers!

(6) To edit the information in any other existing section, click the Edit (pencil) button for that section and make the necessary changes.

(7) To add a new section to your profile, click Add Profile Section and then click the + icon for the type of information you want to add.

(8) Enter the appropriate information for the item you're adding and then click Save.

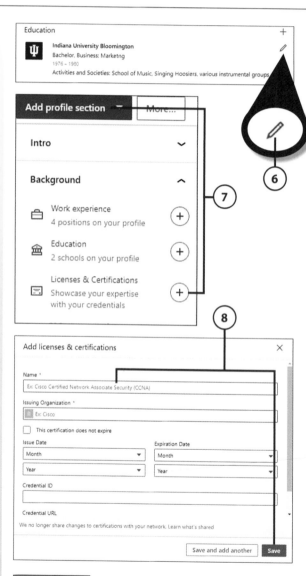

Add or Change a Profile Picture

Profiles with pictures get much more attention than those without. You can easily add a personal picture to your LinkedIn profile.

(1) On your profile page, click the camera icon to open the Open dialog box. (If you've already added a photo, you can change it by clicking the photo and then clicking Change Photo.)

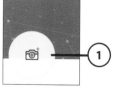

(2) Click Use Camera to take a photo with your computer's camera.

(3) Click Upload Photo to upload an existing photo from your computer.

(4) Select the photo you want to use.

(5) Click the Open button.

(6) You see a preview of your picture as it will appear on the LinkedIn site. Click Crop (activated by default) to edit your picture.

(7) Use the Zoom control to resize your picture.

(8) Use the Straighten control to rotate your picture as necessary.

(9) Use your mouse to drag the picture to better fit within the circle, if necessary.

(10) Click Filter to apply photographic filters to your picture.

(11) Click Adjust to adjust your picture's brightness, contrast, or saturation, or to apply a vignette effect.

(12) Click the Save Photo button. Your photo is uploaded and inserted into your profile.

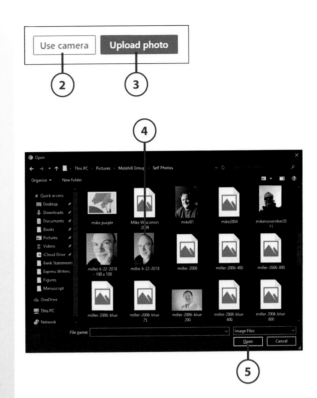

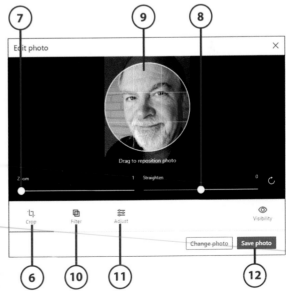

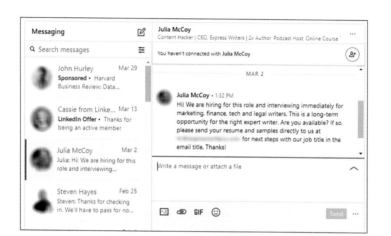

Messaging

🔍 Search messages

John Hurley   Mar 29
Sponsored • Harvard
Business Review: Data...

Cassie from Linke...   Mar 13
LinkedIn Offer • Thanks for
being an active member

Julia McCoy   Mar 2
Julia: Hi! We are hiring for this
role and interviewing...

Steven Hayes   Feb 25
Steven: Thanks for checking
in. We'll have to pass for no...

Julia McCoy
Content Hacker | CEO, Express Writers | 2x Author, Podcast Host, Online Course   •••

You haven't connected with **Julia McCoy**   👤

MAR 2

Julia McCoy • 1:32 PM
Hi! We are hiring for this role and interviewing immediately for
marketing, finance, tech and legal writers. This is a long-term
opportunity for the right expert writer. Are you available? If so,
please send your resume and samples directly to us at
▓▓▓▓▓▓▓▓▓▓▓ for next steps with our job title in the
email title. Thanks!

Write a message or attach a file   ⌃

🖼 ⊂⊃ GIF ☺   Send •••

In this chapter, you discover how to connect with businesses and other professionals on the LinkedIn social network.

→ Finding New Connections
→ Working with Messages and Status Updates
→ Participating in Groups

15

Connecting with People and Businesses on LinkedIn

LinkedIn, like all social media, is all about connecting. In LinkedIn's case, that means business connections—connecting with current and former co-workers, as well as others in your profession.

Business professionals use LinkedIn to expand their list of business contacts, to keep in touch with colleagues, and to keep abreast of developments in their profession. You can use contacts you make on LinkedIn for a number of different purposes, such as finding employment, making a sale, or exploring business opportunities. You also can use LinkedIn to gain an introduction to a specific individual you'd like to know, via connections with mutual contacts.

Finding New Connections

LinkedIn's equivalent of Facebook friends are called *connections*. These are business or professional contacts whom you know and trust. As with

Facebook friends, people on LinkedIn have to accept your invitation before they become connections.

To establish new connections, you can search for current LinkedIn members in your email contacts list, or invite other email contacts to join LinkedIn. In addition, you can search LinkedIn for members who've gone to the same schools or worked for the same employers that you have.

Although you can use the LinkedIn mobile app to search from your phone or tablet, most business professionals use the LinkedIn website for this and similar tasks. The examples in this chapter refer to it, too.

Accept LinkedIn's Recommendations

LinkedIn uses your current connections to recommend other people you might want to connect with. (This is kind of a "friend of a friend" approach.) You can opt to connect with these people if you want.

1. From the LinkedIn menu bar, click My Network.

2. Scroll down to the Recommended for You section and look at LinkedIn's recommendations. Click a person's name to view their profile. *Or...*

3. Click the Connect button to send an invitation to a given person.

Invitations

The people you choose to connect with receive invitations to become connections. If they accept your invitation, you are added to each other's connections list.

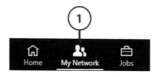

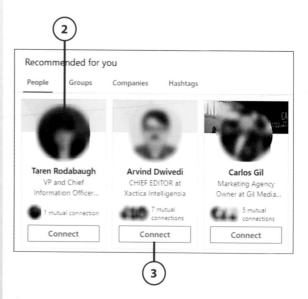

Search Your Email Contacts

Another way to find new connections on LinkedIn is to let the site search your email contacts list for people who are also LinkedIn members.

1. From the LinkedIn menu bar, click My Network.

2. In the Your Contact Import Is Ready section, on the left, click Continue. (You may be prompted to continue before you see the next step.)

3. LinkedIn displays all the people in your email contacts list who also are LinkedIn members. Check the names of those people you'd like to add to your LinkedIn connections list, or uncheck those names you don't want to add.

4. Click the Add Connections button (or, if there isn't anyone to add, click Skip).

5. LinkedIn displays people in your email contacts list who are not yet members of LinkedIn and recommends that you invite them to join. Check the names of those people you'd like to invite.

6. Click the Add to Network button.

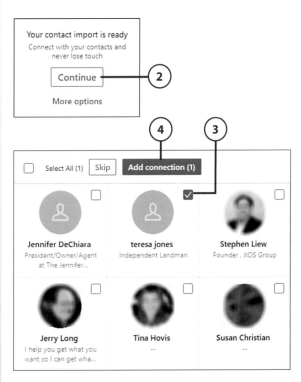

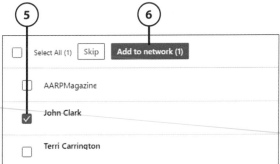

Find Former Co-Workers and Classmates

Another good source of connections are the companies you've worked for and the schools you've attended. LinkedIn helps you find other people who've shared the same employers and schools, so you can add them to your connections list.

(1) From the LinkedIn menu bar, enter the name of the company or school into the Search box and then press Enter.

(2) On the search results page, click People to display people who work at or attended the given company or school.

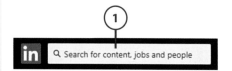

(3) On the toolbar, click to pull down the Connections list and check the type of relationship you want to search for—1st (people you know directly), 2nd (people who know the people you know), and 3rd+ (everybody else).

(4) Click to pull down the Locations list and select a location to search in.

(5) To search for people still employed at a given company, click to pull down the Current Companies list and then select the name of the company.

(6) To filter by other criteria, click All Filters.

7 The search results list changes based on the filters you select. Click the Message button to send a message to anyone who's already a connection.

8 Click the Connect button for any person to whom you'd like to establish a connection.

Working with Messages and Status Updates

LinkedIn offers an internal messaging system. This system enables you to send and receive messages to and from people you're connected to. You also can post status updates that all your LinkedIn connections see on their home pages.

Read and Reply to Messages

LinkedIn's private messaging system is very similar to every other chat or messaging system you've used, except that it works only on and within the LinkedIn site.

1 From the LinkedIn menu bar, click Messaging. (If you have unread messages in your Inbox, the Messaging icon shows a number beside the icon, which indicates the number of unread messages waiting.)

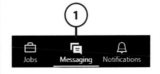

(2) The Messaging panel on the left displays the latest messages you've exchanged; unread messages are in bold. To read a message, click the message header. The message text appears in the center column, along with any replies you've sent.

(3) Reply to a message by selecting that item and then entering your message into the Write a Message or Attach a File box.

(4) Click Send to send the message.

(5) To delete the current message, click the More (three-dot) icon and then click Delete.

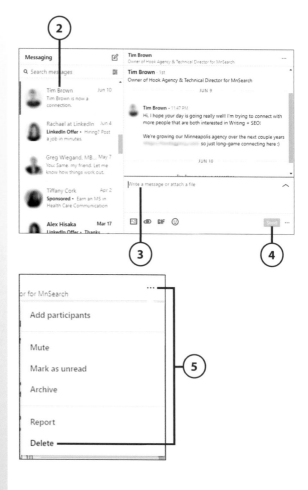

Compose a New Message

It's easy to send a new message to any of your LinkedIn connections.

(1) From the LinkedIn menu bar, click Messaging.

(2) Click the Compose a New Message icon in the left panel.

(3) A new message appears in the center column. Enter the recipient's name or email address into the Type a Name or Multiple Names box.

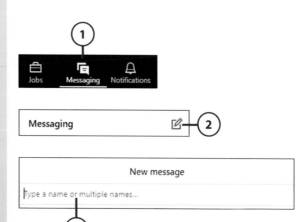

4 As you type, matching connections are displayed; click the name of the person you want to message.

5 Type your message into the Write a Message or Attach a File box.

6 Click Send to send your message.

Post a Status Update

Like Facebook, LinkedIn enables users to post status updates that are displayed in their connections' home pages. (You can also publish longer "articles," but most people use the updates function.) Unlike Facebook, these status updates are not the main focus of the site; LinkedIn is still about personal connections and messages.

That said, you can let your network of connections know about important professional events in your life by posting status updates of this nature. Likewise, your home page features status updates from your connections.

1 On the LinkedIn home page, click Start a Post.

2 Click within the What Do You Want to Talk About? box and type the text of your update.

3 Add a picture to this update by clicking the Image icon and selecting the picture you want.

4 Click the Post button to post this update to LinkedIn.

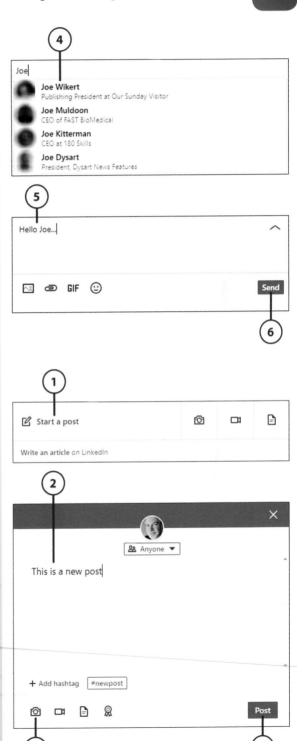

Participating in Groups

Another interesting feature of LinkedIn is its many topic-specific groups. These groups enable professionals to connect with one another regarding specific topics of mutual interest. You can join industry groups, professional groups (such as marketing or advertising groups), alumni groups, and more.

Find and Join a Group

Most LinkedIn groups are public groups, which means anyone can join. Some groups are private, which require the approval of group administrators before an application is accepted.

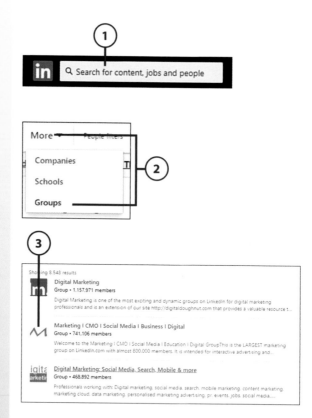

(1) From the LinkedIn menu bar, enter your topic of interest (or group name if you know it) into the search box and press Enter.

(2) Click the More button on the search results page and click Groups.

(3) Click a group's name to view that group's page.

(4) Click the Request to Join button to request an invitation to this group.

Interact with Group Members

Once you've joined a group, you can visit that group's page to interact with other group members.

1 From the LinkedIn menu bar, click My Network.

2 Click Groups on the left side of the page. This displays the Groups page.

3 Click a group's name to open that group's page.

4 Scroll down to read posts in this group.

5 Start a new discussion by clicking Start a Conversation in This Group.

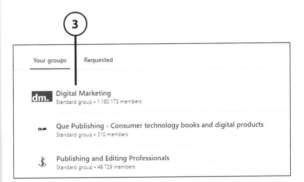

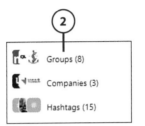

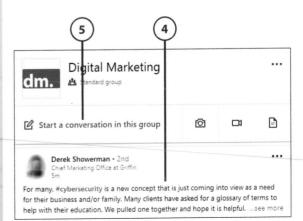

>>>*Go Further*

LOOKING FOR A JOB

Many job seekers today use social networking as a key tool in their hunt for employment. This is important for job seekers of all ages, from recent college grads to older, more experienced members of the workforce.

Employers, too, refer to social networking sites when they have positions to fill, and when they're checking the qualifications of job applicants. Although the full impact of social networking on hiring decisions is difficult to ascertain, LinkedIn reports that close to 30,000 U.S. companies use LinkedIn to find potential employees and that, in any given month, there are more than 3 million job listings posted on the LinkedIn site.

The most direct way to find potential employment on LinkedIn is to search the LinkedIn Jobs database. LinkedIn Jobs features thousands of job listings, organized by industry category; you can search the database by industry, company, title, experience level, date posted, and location.

You access LinkedIn Jobs by clicking Jobs on the LinkedIn toolbar. On the next page, enter the appropriate keywords into the Search Jobs and Search Location boxes; then click the Search button. You can also perform more targeted searches by using the filters on the search results page.

A typical LinkedIn job listing includes a description of the job along with information about the company. Click the Apply button to submit an application.

In addition, you can use your LinkedIn connections to help you find a new position. It's possible that you might have connections—or connections of connections—within the companies for which you'd like to work. You should leverage these connections at a potential employer to learn more about the company, its culture, and its people, and to establish "inside" contacts within the company.

In this chapter, you learn how to use the Instagram app to shoot, share, and view digital photos and videos on your smartphone.

→ Getting Started with Instagram
→ Following Friends, Family, and Others
→ Shooting and Sharing Photos and Videos

Sharing Photos with Instagram

Instagram is different from other social media discussed in this book in that it's primarily a mobile medium. You install the Instagram app on your smartphone or tablet and then use that app to shoot photos and videos, share those items with others, and browse photos and videos shot and shared by your friends and family.

You can use Instagram purely as a camera app, as a photo/video sharing app, or as a viewer for the photos and videos others share with you. You don't have to post any photos or videos to use Instagram; in fact, many people use Instagram solely as a way to view photos and videos shot and shared by other family members.

Getting Started with Instagram

Let's be honest; Instagram is much more popular among younger users than people our age. There are probably lots of good reasons for this, not the least of which is that people in their 20s and 30s shoot a lot more photos and videos (especially of their kids) than do people in their

50s, 60s, and 70s. Instagram lets them shoot and edit their photos and videos on their smartphones and then—in the same app—share those photos and videos with other family and friends.

That said, Instagram is a great way to share family, vacation, and other photos. And even if you don't plan on using Instagram to shoot or share photos and videos you take, it still might be a good idea to install the Instagram app on your mobile device and sign up for a (free) Instagram account.

Download and Install the Instagram App

Instagram is both a mobile app for your smartphone or tablet and a social network. Versions of the Instagram app are available for Apple's iPhones and iPads, Android phones and tablets, and Windows Phone devices. You can download the app (for free) from Apple's App Store, the Google Play Store, or the Windows Phone Store.

After you have the Instagram app installed, you launch the app by tapping its icon on your phone's home screen. The first time you launch the app, you're prompted to either sign in to an existing account or create a new one. Follow the onscreen instructions to proceed.

Mobile Apps

The Instagram app for Android differs slightly from the one for Apple's iPhones and iPads. The examples in this chapter show the Android app; if you're using an Apple device, your screens might look slightly different.

Edit Your User Profile

The next time you open the Instagram app, you're automatically logged in to your account. You can edit the profile information that other users see.

(1) From within the Instagram app, tap the Profile button to display your profile.

2 Tap Edit Profile to display the Edit Profile screen.

3 Tap the item you want to edit or enter, and then enter the necessary information.

4 Tap the check mark when done.

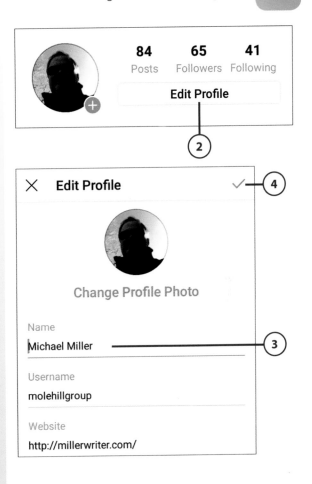

Link to Your Other Social Media Accounts

As part of the initial setup process, you should also link your Instagram account to your other social media. This lets you share the photos you shoot with your Facebook, Twitter, and other online friends and family.

1 From within the Instagram app, tap the Profile button to display your profile.

2 Tap the Options (three-line or gear) icon to display the Options screen.

3 Tap Settings.

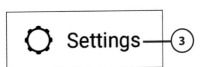

(4) Tap Account.

(5) Tap Linked Accounts.

(6) Tap the social network you want to link to—Facebook, Twitter, Tumblr, or others.

(7) If prompted, enter your sign-in information for this account—typically your email/user-name and password—and tap Authorize App. (If you're already logged in to the social app, you might not have to re-log in here.)

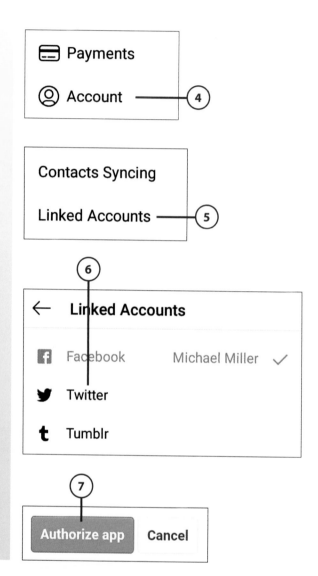

Following Friends, Family, and Others

To view a person's photos, you have to find them and follow them. Their pictures then appear in the photo feed on Instagram's home screen.

Find Facebook Friends

The first place to look for Instagrammers to follow is on another social network—Facebook. If you've linked your Facebook account with your Instagram account, you can quickly and easily turn your Facebook friends into similar connections on Instagram.

1. From within the Instagram app, tap the Profile button to display your profile.

2. Tap the Options (three-line or gear) icon.

3. Tap Discover People.

4. Tap to select the Suggested tab.

5. Next to Connect to Facebook, tap the Connect button.

6. If prompted, tap Grant Access to allow Instagram access to your Facebook account.

7. You see a list of Facebook friends who are also on Instagram. Tap Follow for any friend you want to follow.

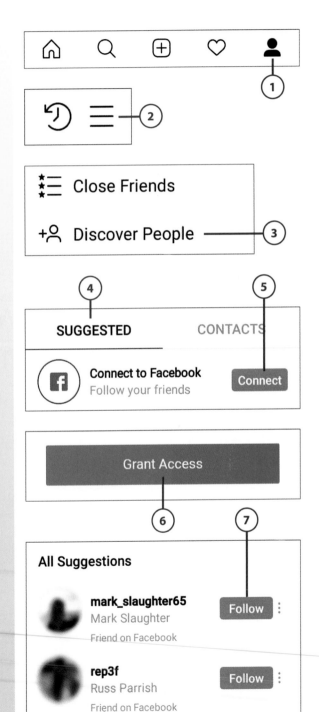

Find Contacts

You can let Instagram search the contacts on your phone for people who are also on Instagram. You can then choose to follow selected contacts.

1. From within the Instagram app, tap the Profile button to display your profile.

2. Tap the Options (three-line or gear) icon.

3. Tap Discover People.

4. Tap to select the Contacts tab.

5. Tap Connect Contacts.

6. If prompted, tap Allow to allow Instagram to access your phone's contacts.

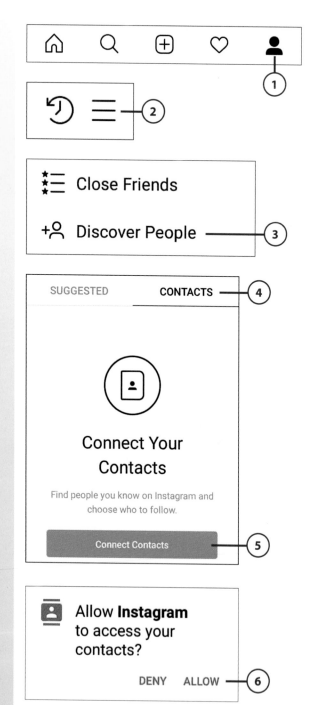

7) You see a list of your contacts who are also on Instagram. Tap Follow for any contact you want to follow.

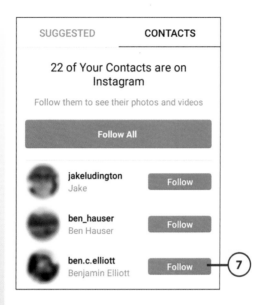

View Friends' Photos and Videos

Photos and videos taken by all the friends and contacts you've chosen to follow appear in the feed that displays on the Instagram app's home screen.

1) From within the Instagram app, tap the Home button to display the home screen.

2) Photos and videos from your friends are listed here, newest first. Scroll down to view more.

3) To like an item, tap the Like (heart) icon.

4) To comment on an item, tap the Comment icon.

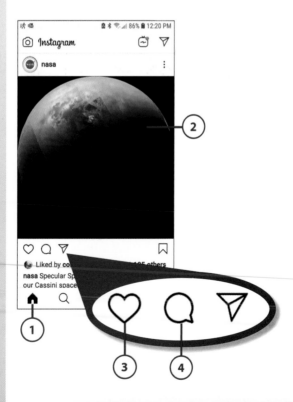

Shooting and Sharing Photos and Videos

You can use the Instagram app to shoot pictures and videos with your smartphone or tablet. You can then edit these photos, apply special effect filters, and share them with your Instagram friends. You can even share your photos to your Facebook or Twitter feeds!

Square Pictures

Unlike your phone's native camera app, Instagram shoots square photos, not widescreen ones—just like your old Polaroids!

Shoot and Share a Photo

(1) From within the Instagram app, tap the + icon.

(2) Make sure that Photo is selected at the bottom of the screen.

(3) Tap the Reverse icon to use the front-facing camera to take a selfie.

(4) Aim your phone and then tap the big round button to take the picture.

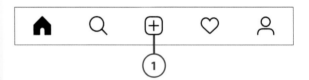

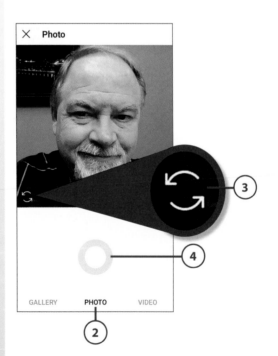

5 You see a preview of your photo. Tap the Filter tab to display a number of photo filters along the bottom of the screen.

6 Tap the filter you want to use.

7 Tap the Edit tab to edit your photo.

8 Tap to select the tool you want— Adjust, Brightness, Contrast, and so on. Scroll left and right to display additional editing tools.

9 Tap Next to display the Share To screen.

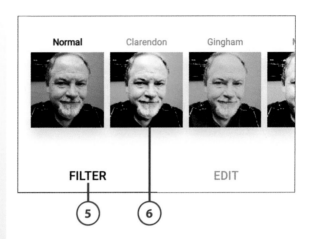

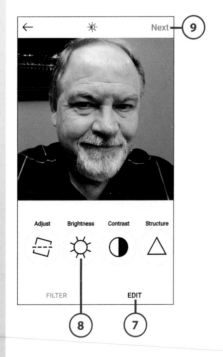

10 Tap the Write a Caption field and enter an optional description for this photo.

11 Tap Tag People to tag people in this photo.

12 Tap Add Location to set a location for this photo.

13 To also share this photo on Facebook, Twitter, and other social media, tap the social network(s) you want to share to. (You have to previously have linked your Instagram account with these social networks, as described in the "Link to Your Other Social Media Accounts" task.)

14 Tap Share to share your photo with your Instagram followers and selected social media.

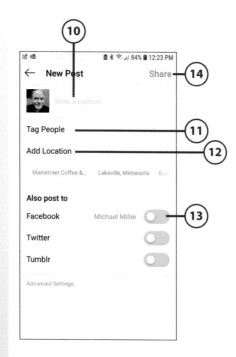

Stories

Instagram lets you create what it calls *stories,* which are photos and videos that are visible to your friends but "disappear" after being viewed. That's beyond our focus here in this chapter, however.

Shoot and Share a Video

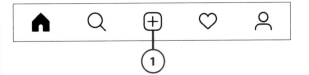

Instagram isn't just for still photos. You can shoot short (3- to 60-second) videos and share them with your followers and social networks.

(**1**) From within the Instagram app, tap the + icon.

(**2**) Tap Video at the bottom of the screen.

(**3**) Aim your phone and then press and hold the big round button to start recording.

(**4**) Release the button to stop recording. Press it again to resume the current recording.

(**5**) When you're done recording, tap Next.

6 You see a preview of your video. If the playback doesn't start automatically, tap the screen to start it.

7 Tap the Filter tab to view a selection of available filters.

8 Tap to select a filter.

9 To choose a thumbnail image to represent this video, tap the Cover tab.

10 Tap to select a cover image.

11 Tap Next to display the Share To screen.

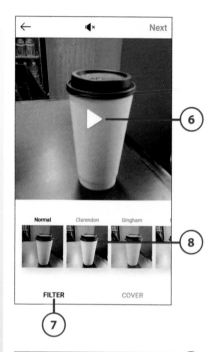

(12) Tap the Write a Caption field and enter an optional description for this video.

(13) Tag anyone in this photo by tapping Tag People.

(14) Set a location for this video by tapping Add Location.

(15) To also share this video on Facebook, Twitter, and other social media, tap the social network(s) you want to share to. (You have to previously have linked your Instagram account with these social networks, as described in the "Link to Your Other Social Media Accounts" task.)

(16) Tap Share to share your video with your Instagram followers and selected social media.

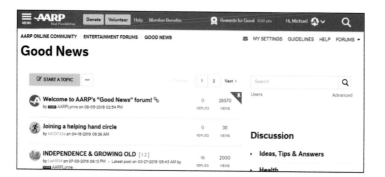

In this chapter, you learn how to interact with like-minded users on special interest message boards.

→ How Message Boards Work
→ Finding Internet Message Boards
→ Reading and Posting to Message Boards

17

Getting Social on Message Boards and Comments Sections

If you have a problem or a question, need help or advice, or want to share on a specific topic, it's time to go online. Facebook and similar social networks are great places to interact with friends and family (and maybe get a little general advice), but when you have a question about a specific topic, it's time to look for websites that offer special interest message boards.

A *message board* is like a primitive social network where you hook up with others who share your same specific interests. They work as collections of messages; you post a message, someone else responds to it, and others respond to that. You end up with wide-ranging discussions from interested posters, one message at a time.

Similar to message boards are the comments sections you find accompanying the articles on many news and special interest sites. Commenting on an online article is a bit like commenting on a message board or Facebook post; you read the article and then type your comments into the text box at the end. Your comments appear alongside those of other readers; you can then comment on others' comments, and they can comment on yours.

How Message Boards Work

Online message boards have been around since before the Internet. They date back to the dial-up Bulletin Board Systems (BBSs) and commercial online services of the 1980s, such as CompuServe and Prodigy. Today, you tend to find them as part of larger websites, typically those devoted to a specific hobby or topic.

Most message boards work in the same fashion. You use your web browser to go to the website and then click or tap the link to message boards, discussion forums, or whatever it is these things are called on that site. You might need to register before you can post; most forums will let you read messages without registering, however. (Registering is as simple as clicking or tapping the Register or Sign Up button and then providing whatever information the site asks for—typically your name or nickname, email address, and desired password.)

Boards, Forums, and Groups

What some people call message boards, others call Internet forums, online comments, or discussion groups.

What you see next is typically a variety of different boards, each devoted to a specific topic. Some boards have sub-boards, focusing on a specific aspect of the larger topic. Click to enter the board of your choice, and you see a list of conversations started by other users. These conversations—called *threads*—revolve around particular subjects and contain messages from multiple users. When you click or tap the subject of a conversation, you see all the messages in that thread, displayed one after another.

On some boards, the oldest messages in a thread are displayed first, with later messages following in order of posting. So if you want to see the latest messages, you have to click or tap to the final page (of a multi-page thread) and scroll to the bottom.

Other boards make it a little easier on you and display the latest messages first. So if you want to know what people are responding to, you need to scroll through the thread to see the older messages.

Messages are typically displayed in self-contained blocks. Each message block contains the poster's name or username, when the message was posted, and often how long the poster has been a member of this particular board. Clicking or tapping a poster's name displays his or her profile information.

When you respond to an existing thread, your message appears at the end. You can also start new threads by posting a new message with a new subject. Other users read your message and respond as they like.

Some boards are moderated, meaning that a person responsible for that board must approve each new message before it is publicly posted. Other boards don't require this pre-approval but still have moderators who try to guide the conversations and weed out off-topic posts.

Most boards don't place a limit on the length of your posts, although shorter is always better when you're communicating online. Some boards let users post photos and links to other web pages; others don't. In general, message boards tend to be heavy on text and light on images.

Archived Messages

Whatever messages you and others exchange on a message board are typically stored, or *archived*, for as long as the message board exists. You can browse or search some message boards and find message threads from ten or more years ago. That makes a message board a terrific long-term information resource. (Threads from many message boards pop up when you search Google for those particular subjects.)

Finding Internet Message Boards

Where do you find Internet message boards that might interest you? Although there are some sites that offer just message boards on a variety of topics, you also can look for websites that focus on your favorite topics. Once you find one of these sites, chances are the site offers message boards for its users.

For example, if you're a dog person, The Dog Forum (www.dogforum.com) connects you with other dog owners and dog lovers to discuss dog grooming, dog training, dog food, and other dog-related issues. (And share dog photos!)

If you're into classic cars, you'll find the Antique Automobile Club's website (www.aaca.org) of interest. Not only do you get news and articles about classic automobiles, you'll also find a thriving community of classic car lovers in the site's message forums—just click or tap the Forums link on the home page.

To find topic-specific websites like these, fire up your favorite web search engine (Google is my search engine of choice), enter the name of your hobby or interest, and click the Search button. Check out the search results for sites that look interesting, and then visit those sites for message boards, discussion forums, or whatever they call their online communities. Chances are the sites you find will have thriving online communities.

You can also check out the more general-interest sites and forums in the following table. These sites have vibrant message forums of particular interest to those of us aged 50 and up.

Online Message Forums

Forum/Website	Web Address	Description
AARP Online Community	community.aarp.org	A variety of forums on topics of interest to people aged 50+, including health, work and retirement, money, travel, entertainment and leisure, and technology
Altdotlife	www.altdotlife.com	A collection of communities revolving around various hobbies and lifestyles, including arts and crafts, cooking, pets, sports, technology, and more
Buzz50	www.buzz50.com	Forums for over-50s, focusing on social interactions, health, pets, food, travel, and more
Chow Community	www.chowhound.com/community	Discussions about cooking, recipes, and more

Forum/Website	Web Address	Description
Discuss Cooking	www.discusscooking.com	Discussion forums for home chefs, with topics for cookbooks, nutrition, special diets, menu planning, and more
Do It Yourself	www.doityourself.com/forum/	A huge number of forums devoted to all manner of DIY projects, including home renovation, gardening, auto repair, interior decorating, and more
eHealth Forum	www.ehealthforum.com	A great source for health-related questions and answers, with forums for addiction and recovery, depression, PTSD, menopause, erectile dysfunction, cholesterol, gout, hemorrhoids, and more
HealthBoards	www.healthboards.com/boards	All manner of forums focusing on specific health issues, including arthritis, back problems, bone disorders, Alzheimer's disease, epilepsy, Crohn's disease, and more
HobbyTalk Forums	www.hobbytalk.com/bbs1/	Discussion boards for all manner of hobbies, including collectibles, model kits, R/C cars and planes, and more
Patient	www.patient.info/forums	Discussion groups targeting specific medical issues, such as depression, anxiety disorders, allergies, diabetes, cancer, and more
Senior Forums	www.seniorforums.com	Discussions on a variety of topics of interest to older users, including retirement living, health insurance, health, family and relationships, entertainment, hobbies and crafts, and photography

Forum/Website	Web Address	Description
Seniors Only Club	www.seniorsonly.club	Separate boards for education and learning, movies and entertainment, philosophy and psychology, reading and writing, science and nature, sports and recreation, food and drink, and more
Simple Living Forums	www.simplelivingforum.net	All about living simply and frugally, with discussion boards for family matters and relationships, emergency preparedness, food and recipes, gardening and farming, health care, organizing your life, personal finance, and more
Zealot	www.zealot.com	All sorts of hobby-related discussion boards for card models, RC cars, model trains and railroads, and more

>>>Go Further

PARTICIPATING IN COMMENTS SECTIONS

Many online news sites offer readers the opportunity to comment on articles via online comments sections. Depending on the nature of the site and its readers, these comments can remain civil and constructive, or devolve into name calling and threats. (It's all too tempting to be an online bully when your comments are anonymous.)

Comments on a news article ——

All Comments (22)   Viewing Options ▾

cbl55 1 hour ago
My condolences to Kieran's family and the Sidwell Friends community. He sounded like a wonderful child.
Like 👍 3   Reply ↰   Link ⇔   Report ⚑

futureexpat 6 hours ago
Tragic proof of the senselessness of terrorism, wherever it happens.
Like 👍 7   Reply ↰   Link ⇔   Report ⚑

To keep the vitriol under control, some sites try to moderate the comments, weeding out those that are too aggressive or personal or just way off-topic. Other sites no longer allow anonymous comments, instead requiring commenters to log in to the site or use their Facebook IDs to comment. And some sites no longer allow comments on articles, thanks to too many offensive and abusive comments in the past.

In any case, reading and participating in these comments sections gives you a feel of how people are responding to what's going on in the world today—or just whether or not they agree with a particular article or position. Comments sections are also good places to blow off a little steam, if you don't mind getting burnt by how others respond to what you say. You definitely need a thick skin to participate in some of these sections; it behooves us all, however, to keep things as civil as possible.

Reading and Posting to Message Boards

Every online message board has a unique look and feel. The processes of reading and posting messages, however, are similar for all sites. The examples show the AARP Online Community forums (community.aarp.org), but the steps outlined here should work for most message boards.

Read and Reply to Messages

After you find a message board or forum in which you're interested, it's a matter of clicking through the layers until you get to the thread you want to read.

(1) Click or tap the general category in which you're interested.

Discussion

- ▸ **Ideas, Tips & Answers**
- ▸ **Health**
- ▸ **Retirement**
- ▸ **Money**
- ▸ **Travel**
- ▸ **Home & Family** —————— (1)
- ▸ **Politics & Society**

2 If there are additional subcategories, click or tap the one within which you want to view all the threads.

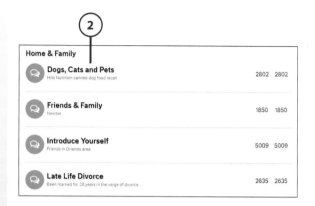

3 The header for each thread displays the subject, number of messages within the thread, original poster, and time/date of the most recent post. Click or tap the subject to view the messages within.

4 If the messages in the thread are displayed in order of oldest first, scroll down the page to view replies to the original message. If the messages are displayed in order of newest first, scroll down to view previous messages.

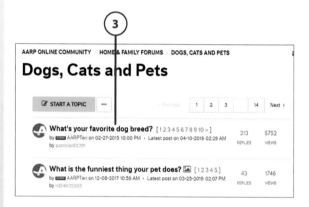

5 If there are enough messages in the thread, newer messages are displayed on additional pages. Click or tap the page number to go directly to that page.

6 To post a message to this thread, click or tap the Reply button to display the post page or pane.

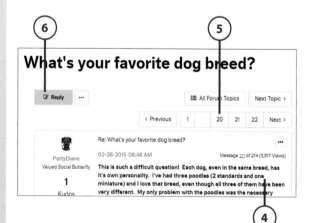

(7) The subject of the thread is already entered into the Subject box. Enter your message into the reply text box.

(8) Click or tap the Post button when done. Your message appears in the thread.

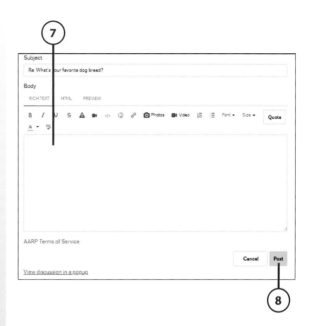

Start a New Thread

If you have a new question to ask or a comment to make that doesn't pertain to an existing subject, you can start a new thread to encourage other readers to interact with you.

(1) Navigate to the specific category in which you're interested.

(2) Click or tap the Start a Topic button to display the post page or pane.

(3) Enter the subject of your message into the Subject box.

(4) Enter the text of your message into the large text box.

(5) Click or tap the Post button. Your message appears as a new thread on the selected board.

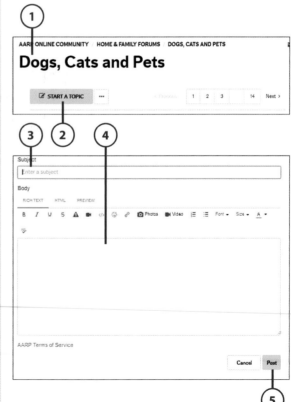

18

Getting Social with Video Chats

Most social media help you connect with friends and family via text messages or photos. That is, you write or upload something and leave it for others to read in their news feeds; it's not real-time interaction.

When you want to get social in person—well, over the Internet, in any case—*video chatting* is the way to go. There are various services available that let you use your computer, smartphone, or tablet to chat face to face with people in real time. It's like the videophones promised to us in the cartoons and movies of the 1950s and 1960s, except it's here today and available over the Internet.

Understanding Video Chatting

Not everyone lives close to family and friends. Even if you do have a close-knit local community, you might find yourself missing loved ones when you're traveling. Just because you're far away, however, doesn't mean that you can't stay in touch—on a face-to-face basis.

This is where video chatting (sometimes called *video calling*) comes in. A video call is a face-to-face, real-time chat over the Internet.

To make a video call, both you and the person you're calling must be connected to the Internet. The video chat uses your device's camera and accompanying microphone to transmit your picture and voice to the other party over the Internet. You see the person you're talking to via his or her camera and microphone, too. Once connected, all you have to do is start talking.

You can use your mobile phone, tablet, or computer to conduct video calls. Smartphones and tablets have cameras and microphones built in, of course; to make a video call with your computer, it must have a webcam built in or attached. (Notebook computers typically have built-in webcams; you'll probably need to connect an external webcam to a desktop or all-in-one PC.)

Video chat works best if you have a relatively fast and stable Internet connection. On slower connections, the picture might get a little choppy or even freeze from time to time.

There are several popular video-chatting services available to you today. If you have an iPhone or iPad, you're probably familiar with Apple's FaceTime, which enables audio and video calls between Apple devices. (FaceTime doesn't work with Android devices or personal computers.) For cross-platform video calls—that is, between devices of any type—the most common choice is Skype, which is owned by Microsoft and works on Windows and Mac computers, as well as iOS and Android mobile devices. Facebook also offers video chatting with your friends on its social network.

All these services work in much the same fashion and let you talk via video to the people you love. It's a great way to stay social when you're online.

>>>Go Further

WEBCAMS

Most notebook PCs have webcams built in. You can use your notebook's built-in webcam to make video calls with Skype and other video-calling services. Because the webcam includes a built-in microphone, you also can use it to make voice calls.

If your PC doesn't have a built-in webcam, you can purchase and connect an external webcam to make video calls. Webcams are manufactured and sold by Logitech and other companies, and connect to your PC via USB. They're inexpensive (as low as $30 or so) and sit on top of your monitor. After you've connected it, just smile into the webcam and start talking.

Video Chatting with Skype

The most popular cross-platform service for audio and video chats is Skype. You can use Skype to conduct one-on-one text chats, audio conversations, and video chats. (This section focuses on video chats.)

To use Skype for video calling on your computer, you must first download and install the free Skype application, available from www.skype.com. To use Skype on your smartphone or tablet, download the free Skype app from your device's app store. (The Skype app is available for both Android and iOS phones and tablets.)

After you have the Skype app installed, you can create your own Skype account. (If you're using Skype on a Windows PC, you also can sign in with your Microsoft account.) The basic Skype service is free and lets you make one-on-one voice and video calls to other Skype users, as well as group audio and video calls. Skype also lets you make audio calls to landline and mobile phones outside the Skype service, but you pay a fee for that service.

This chapter focuses on using Skype on your mobile phone, using Skype's Android app. Operation is similar with Skype's iOS app and on desktop and notebook computers.

Add a Contact

Before you call someone with Skype, you have to add that person to your Skype contacts list. Here's how you do it from Skype's Android app.

1. From within the Skype app, tap to select the Contacts tab.

2. The My Contacts tab is selected by default, which displays all your current Skype contacts. (Select the All tab to view all the contacts on your phone.) Tap the Search icon to display the Search screen.

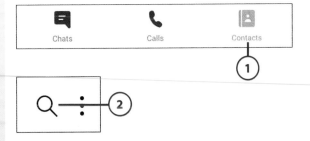

3 Enter the name, email address, or phone number of the person you're looking for.

4 As you type, Skype displays people who match your query. Scroll down to the Skype Directory section and tap to select the person you want.

5 You have to send a contact request to this person. Enter a short message into the Type a Message box.

6 Tap the Send icon to send this message. If the person accepts your request, you'll be added to each other's contact lists.

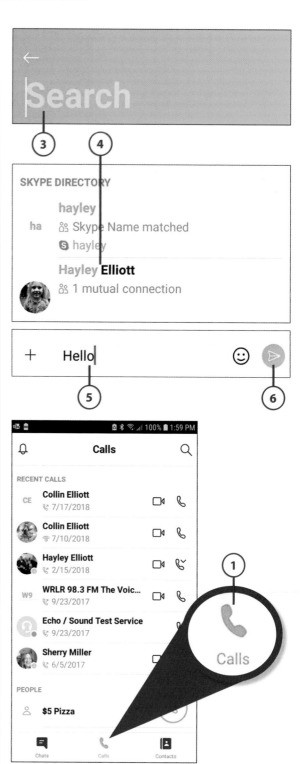

Accepting Contact Requests

Just as you can request someone to be your contact, other people can send contact requests to you. You have the option of accepting or declining any request. Make sure it's someone you know before you accept.

Make a Video Call

The whole point of Skype is to let you talk to friends and family. You can use Skype to make voice-only calls or to make video calls—which are great for seeing loved ones face to face. (You also can send text messages to your contacts via Skype.)

1 From within the Skype app, tap to select the Calls tab.

2 You see a list of recent audio and video calls. Tap the Video icon next a previous call to make another video call to this person. *Or…*

3 Tap the New Call icon to display the New Call screen.

4 Tap the People, Groups & Messages field.

5 Tap the Search field and start typing the other person's name, email address, or phone number.

6 As you type, people who match your query are displayed. Tap the name of the person you want to call.

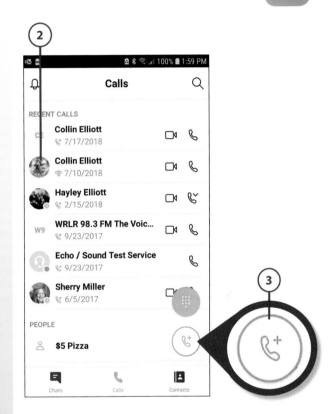

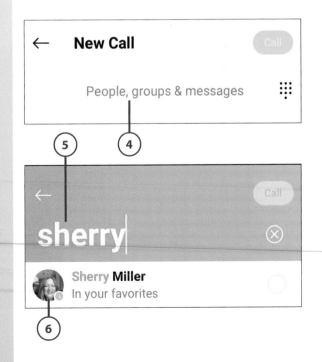

⑦ Tap Call.

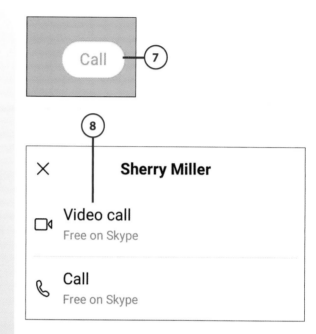

Group Calls

You can make group video calls. Just select more than one person in step 6, and everyone you select will be included in the call—and displayed onscreen.

⑧ Tap Video Call. (To make an audio call, tap Call instead.)

⑨ Skype calls this person. When she answers the call, her live picture appears in the main part of the screen. (Your live picture appears smaller in the corner.) Start talking!

⑩ When you're done talking, tap the screen to display the controls at the bottom and then tap the red "hang up" button to end the call.

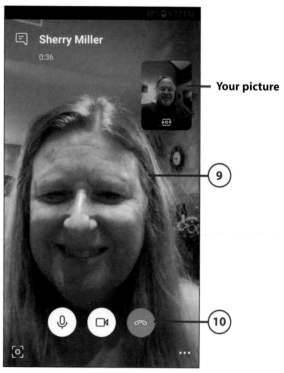

Your picture

>>>*Go Further*

APPLE FACETIME

If you have an iPhone or iPad, and you're talking to another iPhone/iPad user, you can use Apple's FaceTime service for one-on-one video chats. FaceTime works only on Apple devices, so you can't use it with an Android phone or Windows PC. However, it's very easy to use if you have an Apple device.

To conduct a FaceTime call, all you have to do is open the Contacts app and tap a person's name. From that person's contact screen, tap FaceTime. Your phone now calls the other person's phone, and when she answers, you see each other on your respective screens. Start talking until you're done, and then tap the End button.

All   Posts   **People**   Photos   Videos   Marketplace   Pages   Places   Gr

Filter Results

CITY
- Any city
- Burnsville, Minnesota
- Indianapolis, Indiana
- ⊕ Choose a City...

EDUCATION
- Any school
- Ben Davis High School
- Indiana University (Bloomington)
- ⊕ Choose a School...

WORK
- Any company
- Macmillan Publishing
- ⊕ Choose a Company...

MUTUAL FRIENDS
- Anyone
- Friends

Mark Andrew Jones   ✓ Friends ▾   ⋯
Saint Nicholas Episcopal Church, Pompano Beach, Florida
Rector (previously Priest-in-Charge) at Saint Nicholas Episcopal Churc...
Studied School of Theology at Sewanee: The University of the South '10
👥 20 mutual friends

Mark Shaffer   ✓ Friends ▾   ⋯
Allison Transmission Inc.
Purdue
Worked at Allison Transmission Inc.
Studied at Purdue '79

Mark Froelich   👤 Add Friend   ⋯
Indianapolis Fire Department
Works at Indianapolis Fire Department
Studied at Indiana University – Purdue University Indianapolis
👥 9 mutual friends including Jenny Dalton and Jane Ellen Flanders

Mark French   ✓ Friends ▾   ⋯
The Daniel Academy
Teacher at The Daniel Academy
Studied at The Southern Baptist Theological Seminary '98
👥 13 mutual friends

In this chapter, you learn various tips and techniques that help you connect with long-lost friends on social media.

→ Choosing the Right Social Network
→ Searching for Specific Friends
→ Searching for Friends from Your Hometown, School, or Workplace
→ Looking for Mutual Friends
→ Looking for Friends in Facebook Groups

Using Social Media to Find Old Friends

The primary reason most people use social media is to keep in touch with family and friends. I've found Facebook and other social networks to be great places to get back in touch with people I haven't seen in years. I've become newfound "friends" with people I used to work with, old high school buddies, even the next-door neighbor kids I used to play with when I was in grade school. I would have no idea what these people were up to if it wasn't for social media.

How can you use social media to reconnect with old friends, schoolmates, and colleagues? It can be a bit of a detective job at times, but there are techniques you can use to find people you haven't heard from in years. Read on to learn more.

Choosing the Right Social Network

When seeking old friends online, the first thing you have to do is choose the right social network. Some are better for finding certain friends than others.

Start with Facebook

Not surprisingly, Facebook should be your first stop in the search for old friends. It's a matter of size; with more than two billion users worldwide, if your friends are online, they're more likely to be on Facebook than on any other social network.

Facebook offers various ways to find people on its site, which we'll discuss later in this chapter. You can search for people by where they live, their hometown, where they went to school, where they used to work, and more. You also can search by first or last name, of course, as well as search for people who are friends of your Facebook friends—and thus are likely to be old friends of yours as well.

That doesn't mean you'll always find the people you're looking for on Facebook. Even with so many users, not everyone in the world is on Facebook. But it's still the best and first place to look.

Look for Business Contacts on LinkedIn

If you're looking for people you used to work with, LinkedIn might be a better choice than Facebook. LinkedIn lets you search for people by company or industry, so you can easily find people who worked at the same companies you did or who operate within the same industry. For that matter, you can find other people who work or worked at a given company and query them about specific people they may know or have worked with.

Participate in Online Message Forums

If you know a particular person has a favorite hobby, you may be able to track that person down through topic-specific websites and message forums. For example, if you went to school with a guy who liked to build model cars and airplanes, start hanging out at The Clubhouse forums (www.theclubhouse1.net); if your friend played drums in school, try Drumforum (www.drumforum.org). Browse the forums, search the user lists, or even leave a few messages asking about a given person. If you know where to look, you might find the person you're looking for.

And how do you find topic-specific websites and message forums? That's why we have Google. Just do a search on your topic of choice and then click through the search results until you find an interesting site. Chances are that site will have the message forums you're looking for.

It's Not All Good

Other Social Media—Not So Good

Not every social network is as easy to find people on as are Facebook and LinkedIn. For example, I'd never recommend using Twitter to find old friends; it collects only minimal biographical information about users and really isn't designed to facilitate that kind of social connection. Neither is Pinterest, for the same reasons.

Not that you can't find anybody on these other social media, it's just that your odds are a lot less than when using Facebook or LinkedIn. Feel free to try, but don't be surprised if your efforts are less than successful.

Searching for Specific Friends

Sometimes the most effective friend-finding method is the most direct—just use the search function on any social media site to search for a person by name. And sometimes this will work.

Other times, however, the person might be on that site but not so easily found. Imagine, for example, that you're searching for someone named John Brown. A given site's search results may very well turn up the person you're looking for, but you'd never know because of the other several thousand John Browns listed. When you're searching for someone with a common name, it's easy for that person to hide in plain sight.

For this reason, you might want to fine-tune your search by including other information about that person, as we'll discuss in the next section. Search for John Brown, but make sure you're filtering by hometown or high school (or whatever) to narrow your results.

You can include other information in your search query to generate more focused results. Include the person's middle name (if you know it) in the query, along with the person's age or birth date (or birth year, at least), old email address, names of family members, and so forth. The more precise your query, the more exact the results.

Not Everything Can Be Found

You can include all the search criteria you want, but you can only find information that people have actually entered. So if you're searching for an old golfing buddy but that guy hasn't entered golfing as one of his hobbies, you won't get a match.

As an example, I was looking for a woman I used to know when we were students at Indiana University. Just searching for her name among IU alumni didn't work because IU's a very big school that's turned out a lot of grads over the years. I did remember, however, that she used to be a piano major way back when, so simply adding the word "piano" to the query effectively narrowed down the results and identified her. (Turns out she later changed her major from piano to composition and is now a successful professor of composition in California. I wouldn't have known that!)

It can be especially difficult to find women who changed their names when they got married. Some women enter their maiden names as their middle names on Facebook and other social media, so the Sara Jensen you used to know might be listed as Sara Jensen McCready, which means her maiden name actually shows up in a Facebook search. Others, however, don't do this—and thus are harder to find.

You can, of course, search for a partial name—searching just for "Sara," for example. What happens next, at least on Facebook, is a little interesting. Facebook returns a list of people named Sara, of course, but puts at the top of this list people who have mutual friends in common with you. That's a nice touch, as it's likely that your old friend has already made a connection with another one of your Facebook friends.

Past that point, you can then display everyone on Facebook with a single first name. But that's going to be a bit unwieldy, unless your friend has a very, very unique name.

Searching for Friends from Your Hometown, School, or Workplace

In the last section, we discussed fine-tuning your search using other details about a person—where she used to live, where she used to go to school, and so on. Facebook is particularly good at fine-tuning your searches in this manner.

When you're searching for old friends on Facebook, you have the option of filtering your results by a number of key factors, including the following:

- City (current or former)
- School (high school, college, or grad school)
- Employer (current or former)
- Mutual friends

It's a matter of selecting which of these criteria you're looking for and then browsing through the results returned by Facebook.

I discussed how to filter your Facebook search results in Chapter 6, "Keeping in Touch with Friends and Family on Facebook." Revisit that chapter for more details.

Multiple Criteria

To further fine-tune your search, select more than one filter at a time. For example, you can search for people who attended your high school and now live in your current city.

Looking for Mutual Friends

Another way to find old friends is to look for people who are friends of your current friends. That is, when you make someone your friend on Facebook, you can browse through the list of people who are on his friends list. (Other social media work similarly.) Chances are you'll find mutual friends on this list—people that both of you know but you haven't been able to find otherwise.

It's easy to do. Just click or tap your friend's name anywhere on the Facebook site, such as in a status update, to display his profile page. Then you want to click or tap Friends under the person's name to display his Friends page, which lists all of his Facebook friends. When you find a person you'd like to be friends with, click the Add Friend button. That's it.

Mutual Friends

If this process doesn't find the person you're looking for, you still might be able to find him by getting in contact with other people who knew that person. Another friend of an old friend might have more current information than you have. Ask questions of any and all mutual friends—when they last saw or talked to this person, whether they have a current email address or phone number, and the like.

Looking for Friends in Facebook Groups

Another place to search for old friends on Facebook is in Facebook groups. Specifically, look for groups that focus on a particular area of your life—your high school, area of town, place you used to work, general range of years, and so forth. If you're lucky, you may find the person you're looking for as a member of that group. If not, you can always post to the group asking about a given person.

Some examples…

- I went to Ben Davis High School in Indianapolis and graduated in 1976. Unfortunately, there's no group for people who graduated my year, but there is a group called Ben Davis High School Class of 1975. That's close enough to contain a lot of people I used to know and has been a boon for reconnecting with former classmates.

- There's another high school–focused group I belong to, titled "Ben Davis: Where Is *and/or* Do You Remember." This group is focused solely on finding old classmates over a variety of years. It's a great place for posting questions about people I've long lost touch with.

- I belong to several other local groups that have proven useful in finding old friends from my youth. There's Ben Davis Alumni Unite!, Growing Up on the Indy Westside, Indy West Side, Old Time Indy's Long Missed Businesses, and more. Some of these groups are more useful than others; some are just fun places to reminisce about days gone by.

I'm sure there are similar groups for your old high school and town. All it takes is a little searching—and then participating in the group to find friends you used to know.

Find a Group

Learn more about finding and participating in Facebook groups in Chapter 8, "Discovering Interesting Groups on Facebook."

>>>*Go Further*

BEYOND SOCIAL MEDIA

If you're serious about reconnecting with an old friend, don't limit your online search to Facebook and other social media sites. There are other places on the Internet that can help you find specific people.

First, there's Google. It may seem somewhat obvious, but you'd be surprised how many people you can find just by Googling their names. To narrow down the search results, include as much information as possible about that person in your query, and enclose the person's name in quotation marks, like this: "Michael Miller." If you know the person's middle name or initial, include it, too.

Next, there are a number of people search sites on the Web. These sites are designed specifically to help you find individuals; most are free, although some charge a slight fee. The most popular of these sites include

- AnyWho (www.anywho.com)
- PeopleFinder (www.peoplefinder.com)
- Pipl (www.pipl.com)
- Spokeo (www.spokeo.com)
- ZabaSearch (www.zabasearch.com)

Alumni sites also are good places to track down old schoolmates, so check out Alumni.NET (www.alumni.net) and Classmates (www.classmates.com). If your high school or college has an alumni page or website, check that out as well.

Unfortunately, some of the friends you're looking for might have passed on. Some sites, such as FamilySearch (www.familysearch.org) and Tributes (www.tributes.com), offer free access to the Social Security Death Index, which lists more than 90 million deaths in the United States. You can also check out Legacy.com (www.legacy.com), which offers a database of obituaries published in hundreds of local newspapers.

Snapchat

Flickr

YouTube

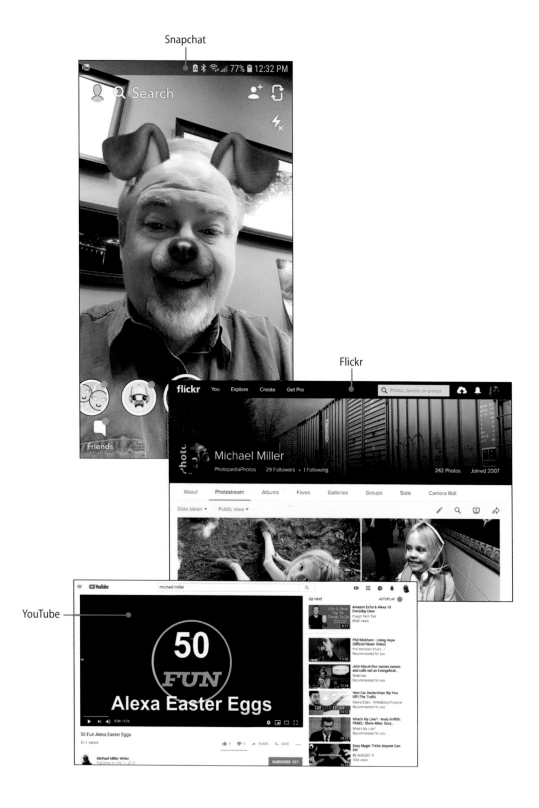

In this chapter, you learn about other social media of interest.

→ Discovering Other Social Networks
→ Discovering Media-Sharing Services
→ Discovering Other Microblogging Services
→ Discovering Mobile-Messaging Media
→ Exploring Other Social Websites

20

Exploring Other Social Media

Facebook, LinkedIn, Pinterest, Instagram, and Twitter are the most popular social media for users aged 50 and up. But they're not the only social media out there. There are lots of other social media, many popular among younger users, that might also be of interest to you.

This chapter briefly examines some of these other social media, many of which are designed specifically for mobile use. Although you might not be interested in some or all of these sites for your use, you might find some of them useful for keeping up with younger members of your family.

Discovering Other Social Networks

Facebook is the largest social network on the Internet today, but there are other social networks, both in the United States and abroad, that appeal to more targeted audiences. Many of these are somewhat country-specific, offering a Facebook-like experience to speakers of a given language.

These other social networks include the following:

- **ASKfm** (www.ask.fm): On this social network for high school and college students, users can ask questions (no matter how embarrassing) of other users and get frank (and hopefully honest) answers. Grownups are not particularly welcome on this network.

- **Badoo** (www.badoo.com): This dating-focused social network is popular in Latin America, Spain, Italy, and France.

- **Qzone** (https://qzone.qq.com): This is the number-two social network worldwide, and the leading social network in China. If you have a lot of friends or relatives in China, it's worth checking out.

- **Reddit** (www.reddit.com): Reddit is an odd bird—a combination of social network, online discussion board, and bookmarking site. It attracts a primarily young, male, tech-savvy audience; many of the most popular topics on the site are technology-related, although you can find just about anything you can think of on the site. The Reddit site is built around a series of topic-oriented communities called *subreddits*, each with its own purpose, standards, and moderator. Although there are tens of thousands of existing subreddits, any user can create a new subreddit as the topic demands.

Reddit ⎯⎯⎯

- **Sina Weibo** (www.weibo.com): This is the number-two social network in China, behind only Qzone.

- **VKontakte** (www.vk.com): Also known as VK, this is the largest social network in Russia. So if you have a lot of Russian friends or family, this is a go-to site.

Discovering Media-Sharing Services

Aside from Pinterest and Instagram, there are a number of media-sharing services online. Many are mobile-only networks; most have mobile apps that let you snap photos or shoot videos on your mobile phone and then share them online with your friends and followers.

The top photo- and video-sharing social networks today include the following:

- **Flickr** (www.flickr.com): Although diminishing in popularity, Flickr remains the largest photo-sharing community on the Web, with more than 50 million active users. It's particularly popular among professional and semi-pro photographers. Because of its large user base, Flickr offers the most opportunities for social networking. Basic membership is free, although paid memberships are available that let users store and share a larger number of photos online. Flickr displays a user's stream of photos (literally, a *photostream*) on its main page; you can search for photos by keyword or browse the most recent uploads, and then share the photos you like with your friends.

- **Fotki** (www.fotki.com): Like Flickr, a free photo-sharing community. You can easily search Fotki for photos by keyword or from a specific member.

- **Photobucket** (www.photobucket.com): Similar to Fotki and Flickr—a free photo-sharing community that lets you search for photos by keyword.

- **Snapchat** (www.snapchat.com): A mobile social network that lets users shoot photos and short videos to share with friends on their smartphones. Unlike other social networks, there is no archived trace of users' activity; shared photos and videos "disappear" 10 seconds after viewing. (You also can augment your photos and videos with filters and overlays, which can be fun.) This app is very popular among younger users.

- **TikTok** (www.tiktok.com): A mobile social network for teens to create and share short (3- to 60-second) music videos and looping videos. TikTok has become immensely popular in a relatively short period of time, with more than 500 million users worldwide.

- **Vimeo** (www.vimeo.com): A video-sharing network, similar to YouTube, but with an additional focus toward business users.

- **YouTube** (www.youtube.com): Owned by Google. YouTube describes itself as "the world's most popular online video community." On YouTube, users upload their digital videos and share those videos with other users. YouTube offers an interesting and ever-changing mix of amateur and professionally produced videos that are easily sharable with friends and followers.

YouTube —

Discovering Other Microblogging Services

A *microblog* is similar to a traditional blog, in that it is a way for creators to broadcast their views and content to a wide, web-based audience. It differs from a traditional blog, however, in that each *micropost* is typically much shorter than a traditional blog post—in some instances, only a sentence or two. Some microblogs consist solely of pictures or videos, with little or no accompanying text. The result is a medium best suited for immediate and direct proclamations, rather than long and involved musings.

Twitter is the Internet's most popular microblogging service—and it pretty much has the market to itself. There is one other microblogging service of note, however, and that's Tumblr (www.tumblr.com). Tumblr is subtly different from Twitter, offering true microblogs, not just a stream of unrelated messages. All of a user's posts are collected on his Tumblr blog page; users can post any combination of text, photo, video, and audio content.

Tumblr

Discovering Mobile-Messaging Media

As more and more older people gravitate toward Facebook, they're driving away younger users. (How hip can a social network be when your grandparents are using it?) Where are all these younger users going?

To some degree, they're scattering, using a mix of Instagram, Snapchat, Twitter, and similar media. But they're also moving toward dedicated mobile-messaging services—social networks that let users send and receive text messages and photos to and from each other's phones. These services are kind of like text messaging on steroids, with the added ability to conference in multiple friends for group chats.

The most popular of these mobile-messaging apps include the following:

- **Kik Messenger** (www.kik.com): This smartphone app lets users send text and photo messages to their friends and families. It's free, has no message or character limits, and is very, very popular among the teen set. Messages can be one-to-one or sent to groups of friends.

- **Viber** (www.viber.com): This messaging app for smartphones enables users to send and receive text, image, video, and audio messages.

- **WeChat** (www.wechat.com): The largest text and voice-messaging app in China.

- **WhatsApp** (www.whatsapp.com): WhatsApp is arguably the most popular mobile messaging app. People use their smartphones to send messages to single recipients or groups of friends, with free unlimited messaging. In other words, it's a great alternative for kids who push up against the limits of the phone company's standard text-messaging plans. WhatsApp is also big internationally, so it's great for use when you're traveling overseas.

Exploring Other Social Websites

There's a whole universe of social media sites and services that we haven't had time to explore in this book. Some are appealing to older users, others are more targeted toward the younger generation.

If you have the time and the interest, you can check out some of these social media sites. Here's a short list:

- **BlackPlanet** (www.blackplanet.com), targeting the African-American community

- **Care2** (www.care2.com), an online community focusing on healthy and green living, especially targeting social activists

- **CaringBridge** (www.caringbridge.org), a nonprofit, charitable network of free websites for people facing serious medical treatment

- **DeviantArt** (www.deviantart.com), a community of artists and art lovers

- **Goodreads** (www.goodreads.com), a website and social community for book lovers and avid readers

Goodreads ————
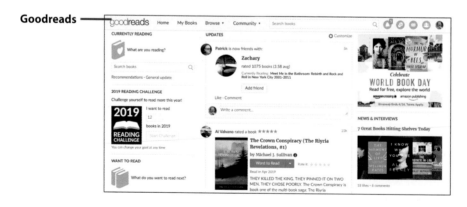

- **LiveJournal** (www.livejournal.com), a social network consisting of user-written journals and blogs

- **Tagged** (www.tagged.com), a service designed to help users meet new people

Glossary

blog   Short for *web log*, a shared online journal consisting of entries from the site's owner or creator.

board   On Pinterest, an online pinboard where images and videos can be virtually pinned.

bookmark   A means of identifying a web page for future viewing or sharing with other users.

connection   On LinkedIn, a professional contact or "friend."

cyberbullying   A form of personal intimidation conducted using social media, mobile phones, and other electronic technologies. Cyberbullies make deliberate and repeated posts that seek to embarrass, humiliate, manipulate, or harm the recipient.

discussion forum   See *message board*.

Facebook   The largest social networking site on the Web, Facebook was launched in 2004 and currently has more than 2 billion users.

fake news   Manufactured stories or posts that present lies and misleading information as if they were actual news stories.

flame war   A heated or hostile interaction between two or more people in an online forum.

Flickr   The Web's largest photo-sharing site, with features for both amateur and professional photographers.

follow   How you connect to other users on various social media sites. When you follow a person, his or her new posts display in your feed or on your home page.

friend   On a social network, another user with whom you communicate. Most social networks enable you to create lists of friends who are authorized to view your posts, photographs, and other information.

friending   The act of adding someone to a social network friends list.

Friendster   One of the earliest social networking websites. Launched in March 2002, Friendster (www.friendster.com) enjoyed a brief period of success before being supplanted by Facebook and other modern social media.

Goodreads   A website and social community for book lovers and avid readers.

group   On Facebook, a topic- or activity-oriented community page where people interested in a given topic or activity can view information and photos, exchange messages, and engage in online discussions about that topic or activity. On the LinkedIn site, it's a user forum dedicated to a topic of mutual interest.

hashtag   A means of indicating an important word in a tweet, similar to identifying a keyword. Hashtags start with a hash character (#) followed by a word or phrase with no spaces. When you click or tap a hashtag, other posts with that hashtag are displayed. (Hashtags can also be used on other sites, such as Instagram and Pinterest.)

identity theft   A form of fraud in which one person pretends to be someone else, typically by stealing personal information, such as a bank number, credit card number, or Social Security number. The intent of identity theft is often to steal money or obtain other benefits.

Instagram   A photo-sharing app and social network that enables smartphone users to shoot and share pictures and short videos.

instant messaging   A means of conducting a one-to-one text communication in real time over the Internet or a closed computer network.

keyword   A word in a search query that describes something you're looking for.

LinkedIn   A social network for business professionals.

malware   Short for *malicious software*, any computer program designed to infiltrate or damage an infected computer. Computer viruses and spyware are the two most common types of malware.

media-sharing network   A social network that enables the sharing of various types of media files (photographs, videos, and music) with other users.

message board   An online space where users can read and post messages on a given topic. Many websites offer message forums for their members.

microblogging service   A web-based service, such as Twitter or Tumblr, that enables users to post short messages to interested followers in a blog-like format.

mobile app   An application for a smartphone or tablet that performs a specific function. Most social networks offer mobile apps for major mobile platforms.

mobile messaging media   Mobile apps, such as WhatsApp, that enable person-to-person text, photo, and/or video messaging in a social setting.

MySpace   An early social network, launched in 2003, eventually supplanted in popularity by Facebook.

news feed   On a social network, a collection of posts or status updates from a person's friends.

Page   On Facebook, a page for fans or followers of an entertainer, celebrity, company, or product.

photo album   On Facebook, a collection of digital photographs or videos organized by some underlying theme or topic.

photo-sharing site   A website where users can upload, store, and share digital photographs with other users.

pin   An item that has been virtually attached to a Pinterest board. The act of placing a pin onto a Pinterest board is called *pinning*.

Pinterest   Launched in March 2010, a visual social network. Users "pin" interesting images on virtual boards, which are then shared with online friends and followers.

profile   A collection of personal information, including photos, contact information, likes and dislikes, and recent posts for a member of a social networking site.

Reddit   A site that combines social networking, online discussion forums, and social bookmarking.

repin   The act of pinning an item that another user has previously pinned to the Pinterest site.

retweet   A tweet forwarded to other Twitter users.

Skype   One of the most popular video chatting services, owned by Microsoft.

smartphone   A mobile phone with advanced computer-like capability, typically including Internet access and the ability to run task-specific apps.

Snapchat   A mobile social network that enables the sharing of pictures and videos that are automatically erased ten seconds after viewing.

social media   Websites, services, and platforms that people use to share experiences and opinions with each other. The most common social media include social networks, social bookmarking services, and microblogs.

social network   A website, such as Facebook or LinkedIn, where users can form communities with like-minded people and share details of their lives with friends, family, fellow students, and co-workers.

spyware   A malicious software program that obtains information from a user's computer without the user's knowledge or consent.

status update   A short post from a member of a social networking site, conveying the user's current thoughts, actions, and such.

subreddit   A topic-oriented community on the Reddit site.

tag   The act of identifying a friend in a status update or uploaded photo.

Tumblr   A microblogging service, launched in 2007, that enables users to post short text or image messages to their own "tumbleblogs," which other users can then follow online.

tweet   A short, 280-character post on the Twitter social media network. Also used as a verb, "to tweet."

Twitter   A popular microblogging service, launched in 2006, where users post short text, photo, and video messages ("tweets") of no more than 280 characters for other users to follow.

unfollow   To no longer follow a given person on a social network.

video chat   A real-time, face-to-face chat between two people, using their computers or smartphones and built-in cameras or webcams.

viral   Achieving immense popularity via word of mouth on the Internet.

website community   A website designed to promote a community around a specific topic. Most website communities feature topic-specific articles and other content, along with discussion boards, chat rooms, and the like.

WhatsApp   One of the most popular mobile messaging services.

YouTube   The Internet's largest video-sharing community, where members upload and view millions of video files each day.

Index

Symbols

Answers to Your Technology Questions

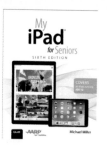

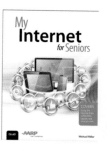

The **My...For Seniors Series** is a collection of how-to guide books from AARP and Que that respect your smarts without assuming you are a techie. Each book in the series features:

- Large, full-color photos
- Step-by-step instructions
- Helpful tips and tricks

For more information about these titles,
and for more specialized titles, visit
informit.com/que

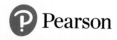